Praying
the Movies

Praying the Movies

the Movies

Daily Meditations from Classic Films

EDWARD McNULTY

GENEVA

Geneva Press
Louisville, Kentucky

Book design by Sharon Adams
Cover design by designpointinc.com

First edition
Published by Geneva Press
Louisville, Kentucky

This book is printed on acid-free paper that meets the American National Standards Institute Z39.48 standard. ♾

PRINTED IN THE UNITED STATES OF AMERICA

Library of Congress Cataloging-in-Publication Data
McNulty, Edward.
    Praying the movies: daily meditations from classic films / Edward McNulty.—1st ed.
      p. cm.
    ISBN 0-664-50155-9 (pbk. : alk. paper)
    1. Meditations. 2. Motion pictures—Religious aspects—Christianity—Meditations.

BV4832.2 .M377 2001
242—dc21   00-061762
  02 03 04 05 06 07 08 09 10 — 10 9 8 7 6 5 4 3 2

Contents

Acknowledgments

Many of the devotions in this book appeared in the author's monthly film magazine *Visual Parables;* two appeared in the quarterly journal *Reel to Real.* Although the previously published devotions have been revised considerably, we are grateful to the original publishers for permission to use them in this book.

The quotation by Malcolm Boyd is from his book *Are You Running with Me, Jesus?,* published by Holt, Rinehart & Winston, 1965. We thank the author for permission to use the quotation and for his words of encouragement to us for writing this book.

Introduction

M ost people regard movies as just a popular
form of entertainment. This view is shared
by many church leaders, too many of whom regard
what is showing at the local theaters as either irrele-
vant or contrary to their work of spreading the
gospel. Cultural elitists dismiss movies as mindless
escapism, and fundamentalist Christians damn
movies as godless garbage. Although agreeing in part
with much of the harsh criticism hurled against
Hollywood, I take a different tack in this book. I
believe that *some* filmmakers are interested in more
than just making money—that a few are attempting
to explore the world beneath the surface appearances
of life. As genuine artists, they invite us to explore
the pain and the joy of being human, to look deeply
into ethical issues and dilemmas, and at times to
enter into worlds far different from our everyday
experience. Their works are the ones that inspired
this anthology of meditations built around film
scenes. I believe that such films help us to understand a little better what it is to be a human being
and, in a few cases, even to see a little more clearly
the emerging kingdom of God.

Years ago I was enchanted by this Malcolm Boyd prayer-meditation in his popular book *Are You Running with Me, Jesus?*:

> Sitting in the theater, I can scarcely wait for the lights to dim.
> —Here I am in my anonymity. I feel shut off from every distraction. The screen is remote, up there, and I'm down here, able to relate or not relate to it as I choose.
> —The film has begun. It is telling a story, and concerns persons. Now I recognize myself. I'm up there, too, Jesus, involved in trying to make a decision. It's painful and I'm suffering.
> —I feel the closeness of other persons near me in the theater. I'm not suffering alone. We are so naked, Jesus, sitting here together and seeing ourselves (and each other) up there. Only the story isn't up there anymore. It's here.
> —When the lights come up, and the movie has ended, will we remember anything of our closeness, Lord, or will we all be sitting quite alone? At first I wanted both escape and communion inside this theater. Now I know I can't escape, Jesus, and also how much I need communion.[1]

I was very excited when I first read Father Boyd's words. Here was someone who felt the way I did about movies, someone who looked forward to the beginning of a film, not just for entertainment—though that is always a factor—but for involvement in the story of other people as they make decisions and face opposition

---

1. Malcolm Boyd, *Are You Running with Me, Jesus?* (New York: Holt, Rinehart & Winston, 1965), p. 77. Used by permission of the author.

and danger and sometimes even death. Here, too, was expressed that paradox of being alone amidst a crowd of strangers, yet also of being bound together by what was unreeling up there on the screen.

I like to read devotional as well as theological books, but some of my most insightful and inspirational moments have come while watching such films as *Grand Canyon, Midnight Cowboy, Smoke,* or *Wild Strawberries.* Before reading Father Boyd's meditation, I had been using films as sermon illustrations and with youth in my parish, and, when I could find a group to pay the rental costs, showing 16-mm versions at special film series for discussion. But this was mostly an affair of the head, a matter of discovering and analyzing theological and ethical themes in the films and relating them to the Scriptures and to life. In *Are You Running with Me, Jesus?,* Father Boyd was showing me that films could also inspire prayer and meditation. In fact, the prayer quoted above is but the introduction for his meditations on eight specific films, ranging from the superserious, such as *Citizen Kane* and *The Silence,* to the seemingly frivolous yet insightful French comedy *Mr. Hulot's Holiday.*

The book you now hold in your hands is a response to Father Boyd's practice of praying the movies. Older readers might also detect the influence of another devotional gem from that same bygone era, Robert Raine's wonderful anthology of readings from a wide variety of sources—plays, novels, memoirs, essays—to which he added relevant Bible verses and a prayer. Entitled *Creative Brooding,* this exciting collection has been a mainstay for me through the years. Sometimes I use it for my own meditation, and very frequently it is the book I turn to when I want a challenging devotion for a group.

Today a great many people, some within but many more without the church, find in a good film satisfaction and meaning similar to that once found in an essay, novel, poem, or sermon. Although film is mainly "just entertainment" for most people, for a growing number, both young and older adults, it provides food for thought, patterns for relating to others, values to strive for and assimilate, and mediated experiences of relating with unusual people in familiar and exotic settings. After *Forrest Gump* opened in the summer of 1994, a minister colleague told me that her twenty-something son was urging her to see the film, saying to her, "Mom, this film told me about my life!"

A number of years ago, an *Esquire* magazine cover story referred to movies as "the religion of the young," with the movie theater serving as their church. (The cover illustration was a picture of Manhattan's St. Patrick's Cathedral onto which was attached a theater marquee.) Joseph Campbell, in his scintillating televised conversations with Bill Moyers (*The Power of Myth*), suggested that movies are the source of mythology for today's children and youth. I know that this was true for my five young children during the heyday of the first *Star Wars* trilogy. Therapist and movie buff Geoffrey Hill follows this up in considerable detail in his fascinating book *Illuminating Shadows: The Mythic Power of Film*, pointing out in detail the mythic motifs in such surprising films as *It's a Wonderful Life*, *Shane*, and *Trip to Bountiful*. Whether or not one can accept all of his claims about film, most observers would agree that it is no exaggeration to say that there are more young adults gathered in the Friday or Saturday night theater congregation than in our church buildings on Sunday morning. Something in film holds a powerful attraction for them that is strong enough for them to get up, turn off their VCRs and TVs, climb into their cars, and pay a small fortune to see the current film everyone on TV talk shows is promoting or commenting on.

Even for some of us who are still members of the old-style churches, film sometimes serves as another means of encountering God or some aspect of transcendence that can transport us out of our normal setting and enlarge our vision or challenge our accepted mores. I will never forget the first time I saw Franco Zeffirelli's *Brother Sun, Sister Moon* at a theater. My family had not wanted to see a movie "about an Italian guy," so I sat alone in the theater—and yet I wasn't alone. I was with young Francesco as he struggled with his demons; I wandered the bright red poppy-strewn fields of medieval Italy with him and heard lovely Clare declare how she preferred the "mad" Francesco who spoke of peace and love to the "sane" young man who, armor-clad, had ridden off to kill or be killed in war. The combination of exquisite color photography, fine performances by the young actors, haunting music by Donovan, and Zeffirelli's masterful direction led me to a spiritual high that made it difficult to sleep that night. (Unfortunately, I probably made up 10 percent of the audience. Few others turned out that night, or any other, to watch Zeffirelli's film, and so it was a financial failure.) Years later, when I was privileged to visit the old church where Francis had first heard Christ call him, St. Damiano's just outside the walls of Assisi, I experienced a similar feeling, but, surprisingly, not nearly as intense as that while watching Zeffirelli's story of the little saint unfold on the screen. The power of a well-told story acted out by flesh-and-blood people is greater than an empty stone building, no matter how hallowed.

The following collection of scenes from films have lifted my spirit in similar ways. I chose the theme of grace because I believe that *grace* is the word that we first need to hear. Not sin, guilt, or judgment, but grace. The church has been too quick to utter the former so often and so shrilly that the world seldom associates the word *grace* with, or even expects it from, the church. This is sadly evident in that the novelist and filmmaker often use a clergy figure or congregation as a symbol of judgment and/or hypocrisy, as we see in films ranging from *Sadie Thompson* to *Elmer Gantry* to *Bad Girls.*

Too many times real-life church leaders seem bent on proving that the Hollywood church stereotypes are true. They have been very vocal in their harsh judgments of sin and sinners, of "Hollywood" and "Hollywood trash." Occasionally a leader can drum up enough frenzy and resentment that his followers will picket a film, as in the case with Martin Scorsese's *The Last Temptation of Christ.* (Indeed, a self-styled Mississippi media watchdog spent a million dollars on ads and a kit mailed to churches to combat Scorsese's film!) Seldom do church leaders marshal any support for a so-called good film. In 1973, *Brother Sun, Sister Moon,* filled with just the spirituality espoused by the churches, died at the box office, as have many other worthy films.

If this were a scholarly biblical or theological essay, I would give a long definition of grace and perhaps trace its history and use in the Scriptures. There is a place for such carefully researched studies, but I would prefer that readers come to their own definitions after reading (or viewing) the episodes described in this book. The Hebrew word translated as "grace" can also mean "favor" or "mercy" ("tender mercies" in the King James translation—also the title of one of my favorite films), and the Greek word means "free gift." But grace is far more than this. These thirty-one instances of grace show how rich and varied it can be, the inner meaning of which defies any attempt at abstract definition. As these silver-screen moments of grace demonstrate, the former slave-ship captain was right when he sang "Amazing grace, how sweet the sound." Grace *is* amazing because, when it appears, it is indeed unexpected, unmerited, and thus sweet indeed.

Ways to Use This Book

This book can be used by readers for their own devotions while alone, or it can be used with a group, perhaps at a film viewing or a retreat. It would be fun to use the book in conjunction with a VCR, with the tape of the film cued up to the scene described in the text. The Scripture passages included are suggestions; readers are encouraged to look for other passages that might speak more directly to their hearts or reflect better the meaning of the film scene to them. The questions also are suggestive, intended to stir the mind as well as the imagination so that readers will enter more fully into the situations of the film characters—or, better, that the film characters and their decisions will relate to the reader's situation. One or more hymns, themselves worthy of study, are suggested because some of the words of the verses connect with a theme in the film. If yours is a group setting, you will need to have hymnals on hand. A word of caution for group use: Be sure that you—or whoever is leading the group—have seen the entire film. Not only will you know the context of the scene better than by reading just this introduction; you will also see any of the objectionable parts to which someone in the group might raise objections. You do not want any surprises in this regard.

You also need to be aware of the FBI warning at the beginning of home videos. Take this warning seriously, because the FBI and the motion picture industry do. To make sure that your use of the videos with groups is within the guidelines of the law, write to the Motion Picture Licensing Corporation at 5455 Centinela Avenue, Los Angeles, CA 90066-6970. Phone (800) 462-8855, or visit their website at www.mplc.com for more information.

I envision a leader opening with some or all of the introductory material from this book. Or, if this way of beginning seems too intrusive because of the nature of the group or the place of showing the film, the material could be used at the conclusion of the discussion. My experience of setting up a film series at a theater suggests that about a third of a film audience will stay to discuss a film. These are people who want to share an insight received from the film and to hear what others think of it. Many times they have already seen the film, the discussion being their main reason for coming to your showing. I am frequently amazed by how much collective insight resides in a group, the discussion becoming for myself and many others an experience similar to what the New Testament writers call *koinonia*, a teachable moment. Many times someone has asked me the meaning of some act or symbol in a film we have just watched. Generally I refer the question to the group, and almost always at least one person is able to provide a helpful answer, sometimes more insightful than what I might have said. I always tell film groups that "all of us will see more than one of us." A sign of Christian community is this helping each other "to see." A concluding devotional moment probably would be acceptable even to those not connected with a church. There have been some discussion sessions so exhilarating, so uplifting, that I wish I had been prepared then to end with a prayer and/or Scripture passage. It would have been a fitting climax, similar to the practice of the Old Testament patriarchs of building a rock altar to commemorate an encounter with the Divine.

Even more, I envision readers going on beyond the limited vision of the author to make their own connections between the secular and the sacred in the movies they see. This has been the most satisfying result of my film seminars and workshops—to have someone come up and say, "You know, from now on I will never see movies in the same way. You've helped me view them with new eyes." If the Spirit speaks to you, I hope that you will write down your own (and the Spirit's) observations and prayers, and will find occasion to share them. When we feel that a work of a filmmaker has blessed us, may we not only *think* about the movie, but also *pray* about it as well.

A Note on Films with Objectionable Parts

I am well aware that most films are too flimsy or shallow to inspire prayer. Only a fraction of the three or four hundred films released each year deal honestly with an important issue or offer a significant insight into relations with God and neighbors. Far too many films, instead of leading to prayers of thanksgiving, more properly move us to utter prayers of anguish: "Good God, get me out of here! Why did all those people listed at the film's end waste their time and talents on such rubbish!" Or maybe it should move us to utter a prayer of confession: "O God, forgive us and the filmmakers for squandering so much of your precious time, talents, and treasures on such trash!" However, that fraction of Hollywood's output, that "saving remnant" of the three or four hundred film releases, can make all the difference in the world. They are what keep those of us concerned with seeing God at work beyond the pages of Scripture coming back to the theater in a spirit of hope and expectancy.

The films in this book were carefully selected, but not on the basis of their ratings. Many of the films are R-rated; some have scenes containing violence, vulgar language, or nudity and sexual situations. These films, however, were made by men and women with a vision and not by those out to exploit these elements. In some cases I wish the filmmaker had not included certain words or actions, but I refuse to turn away from a film because some of my sensibilities are offended. To do so would be to miss out on so much that is good in the films. To borrow a concept from the apostle Paul, we have in film great "treasure" (a gospel insight) but in "earthen vessels." Just as Jesus did not turn away from the R-rated and even X-rated people whom he met, so we should not back away from an R-rated film. Such films contain elements that we deplore alongside nuggets of gospel gold, scenes of beauty and inspiration that can enrich our understanding of faith and life.

Let us then dare to pray the movies, believing that in them God can speak a word of grace to us and to the world. A case in point: one of the most violent and vulgar films of 1994 is Quentin Tarantino's *Pulp Fiction*, yet it is one of the most theologically oriented films I have ever seen (whether by intent or by accident, I do not know). Centered on several gangsters and a boxer, the film tells several stories of grace amidst a sordid world of drugs and criminal activity.

One of the characters rides to freedom on a motorcycle named Grace, and another, a hired killer, is so transformed by what he interprets as a miracle that he gives up his profession and vows to follow where God is calling him.

There are many such films of integrity produced by that "saving remnant" of Hollywood uncorrupted by Mammon or Baal. Just as Abraham bargained with Yahweh for the salvation of Sodom and Gomorrha ("Suppose there are fifty righteous within the city . . . forty . . . twenty . . . suppose ten are found there?"), so we must look, among the four hundred or so new films released each year, for those "twenty . . . or ten" that redeem Hollywood Gomorrha and make filmgoing the worthwhile, sometimes even spiritual, experience we crave. Each year one or two dozen films are released that are filled with intellectual and spiritual nourishment. Some make it to the theaters. An equal or greater number, judged as "not commercial enough" by distributors who must focus on profits, are shown in small art-house theaters where people congregate who love films for more than the escape they provide. Still other films go right to the video stores and libraries where they await the person fortunate enough to discover them. These are the films I love to write about, the films I chose for this book. Such are the films that we can in good conscience meditate on, despite their flaws, and even, when the Spirit moves us, pray—if we develop "eyes that see and ears that hear."

1. Life Is to Give
Les Miserables (1935 version)

How shall we sing the LORD's song
  in a foreign land?

Psalm 137:4 (RSV)

Happy are those whose transgression is forgiven,
  whose sin is covered.

Psalm 32:1

"Truly I tell you, today you will be with me in
Paradise."

Luke 23:43

"And the king will answer them, 'Truly I tell you,
just as you did it to one of the least of these who
are members of my family, you did it to me.'"

Matthew 25:40

Introduction

Jean Valjean, hero of the excellent 1935 film version of
Victor Hugo's novel *Les Miserables*, could well join in
the Psalmist's plaintive cry, "How shall we sing the
Lord's song in a foreign land?" The Frenchman was
cruelly torn from his family and home for many years
when he was caught stealing a loaf of bread to feed his
starving niece. Sentenced to be an oarsman in a galley,
during the long years of back-breaking toil he was
reduced to the level of a brute by the sadistic cruelty of
the guards. "The Lord's song" within him was dis-
placed by his screams of agony and despair and the
bitterness of the injustice of it all.

Released at last, he could find no work or shelter
because of his yellow ex-convict's passport. Every door

was shut in his face, until one stormy night when he was directed to the home of the local bishop.

The Scene

There is a loud knock on the door. Against the wishes of the housekeeper, the clergyman invites Jean in. When the suspicious servant sets out their old dinnerware, the bishop orders that their best silver plate be used. The clergyman treats Jean to a fine meal as if his unkempt guest were a person of high rank. Jean is taken aback by such unexpected treatment; nevertheless, during the night, the ex-convict sneaks off with a bag stuffed with the bishop's silver dishes.

Caught the next day, Valjean is brought back by the gendarmes to face the bishop. When the old man asks them, "Didn't he tell you that the silver was a gift?" the chief officer replies that he did, but that, of course, they had not believed him. To their surprise, and Jean Valjean's, the bishop says that they were indeed gifts, and then addresses his guest, "Why did you leave so early? You forgot to take these two candlesticks." Going over to the mantle, he takes the two silver candlesticks and offers them to Jean. The two policemen leave, and the puzzled Jean Valjean asks if he is really free to go. The bishop muses aloud whether anyone is really free and dismisses his new friend with the admonition to remember that "life is to give, not take." The bishop tells Jean that this day he has claimed his soul and asks him to do likewise for someone else.

They are words that the former convict will never forget, for when he leaves the bishop's house, he pauses at a roadside shrine to pray, obviously beginning the long journey of transformation. At that moment he feels at the core of his being the joy expressed by the writer of Psalm 32: "Happy are those whose transgression is forgiven, whose sin is covered."

Reflection on the Scene

We can never tell what effect our words or unexpected acts of kindness will have on another person. It might be difficult to see Christ "in the least of these," especially if that person is as unkempt looking as Jean Valjean or has injured or threatened us. But this story of the bishop's kindness and Luke's story about Jesus and the thief on the cross remind us that when we become channels of God's grace, nothing is impossible. Like the crucified thief, the seemingly depraved Jean Valjean received grace at the time of his greatest need, thanks to an elderly clergyman who valued a human life far more than he did his silver dinnerware.

The bishop took a risk. Some might call him foolish, perhaps even aiding and abetting a known criminal. However, the bishop, like the Lord whom he emulated, saw in the wretched man brought back by the police not a depraved criminal but a child of God. That child of God he thought well worth taking a chance on, even to the point of telling a lie for him and seemingly throwing away his best silver pieces. What a difference such love can make in the recipient's life!

For Further Reflection

1. With whom in the story do you identify: Jean Valjean or the bishop? Or maybe the suspicious housekeeper or the gendarmes?

2. When and where have you seen such grace in the lives of others? When and where have others seen such grace flowing through you? What are those moments in your relationship with others that could be turning points, turning dis-ease and brokenness into health and wholeness?

3. Can you think of a time when you were the recipient (or the conveyer) of such grace? What did you expect from your wrongdoing or shortcoming? How did you feel when you did not receive what you deserved? Is that not what grace is—the difference between what we deserve and what we receive at such moments?

4. Why do such actions as the bishop's have a profound impact on the recipient, as compared with a sermon or words of advice? Is it partly because the action shows that the bishop is on Valjean's side?

5. How can this story help you deal with others who wrong you? Can you think of someone whom you've given up on as being too far gone to ever change? What do the stories in Luke and the film suggest you should do?

HYMN: "There's a Wideness in God's Mercy" or "Depth of Mercy! Can There Be"

A Prayer

Gracious and amazing God, you created us in your image, and you continue to seek us out, even when we turn away from you and journey into a far country. You loved Jacob the Grasper, Jonah the Runaway, and Peter the Denier. Gracious God, whose grace is still "so amazing, so divine," grant us your loving insight so that we might see what is valuable within ourselves and within the most unlikely of your wayward children. As you have given so much love to us, may we in turn give such love to others, even risking such love on those who seem unworthy. This we ask in the name of him who for us gave his love, and his very life, on the cross, even Jesus Christ, our Lord. Amen.

2. Spilled-Glasses Grace
Charly

Keep me as the apple of the eye;
    hide me in the shadow of thy wings;
from the wicked who despoil me,
    my deadly enemies who surround me.

They close their hearts to pity;
    with their mouths they speak arrogantly.
They track me down; now they surround me;
    they set their eyes to cast me to the ground.
They are like a lion eager to tear,
    as a young lion lurking in ambush.

Psalm 17:8–12 (RSV)

Then he poured water into a basin, and began to wash the disciples' feet, and to wipe them with the towel with which he was girded.

John 13:5 (RSV)

Introduction

In the 1968 film *Charly*, Cliff Robertson plays a mentally retarded worker at a bakery. His coworkers pretend to be his friends, but almost everyone mocks him and plays cruel jokes on him. Despite his mental condition, Charly enrolls in night school to try to learn to read because his mother has instilled in him a strong desire for learning. His teacher, Alice, a clinical psychologist associated with a research team at the local university, treats Charly with dignity and kindness. Impressed by his deep desire to learn, she recommends Charly as a good candidate for an experimental operation designed to increase human intelligence.

As part of the experiment, Charly competes against Algernon, a laboratory mouse whose intelligence was greatly enhanced by the operation. Mouse and man are to figure out the way though a maze—Algernon's in a box, and Charly's on paper. But despite Charly's operation, Algernon continues to beat the human. Day after day Charly looks up in disappointment to see that the little mouse has arrived first at his goal. But then one day, when Charly is about to quit the experiment for good, he wins. Finally he knows that the operation was a success, that he is now smarter than a mouse!

Charly continues to increase in intelligence each day. At the bakery his coworkers are surprised when he is able to learn how to operate the dough-mixer. But as Charly's intelligence grows, far surpassing theirs, his so-called friends soon grow uneasy around him and arrange to have him fired. Hired full-time now by the university project, Charly quickly masters reading, writing, and arithmetic, and soon is studying higher mathematics, physics, biology, and philosophy.

The Scene

One night Charly is at a crowded restaurant. Above the noise of chatter and the clinking of silverware and glasses he hears a loud crash, the sound of breaking glasses. Cheers mixed with laughter arise from the patrons. Looking around, Charly sees that a busboy has spilled a tray of glasses. The boy stands there for a moment, confused by the crash and the laughter and unfriendly cheers that are obviously aimed at him. Earlier Charly had noticed the almost vacant look in the boy's eyes, so he recognizes himself as he had been a few scant weeks ago. He well knows the feeling of hurt and confusion sweeping through the boy at that moment.

The boy stoops down and clumsily tries to gather up the glasses and the shards of the broken ones. The scornful sounds of the boss and of the crowd continue—until Charly walks over to the boy. Charly, without a word, stoops down and helps the young man clean up the mess. Instantly the crowd falls silent. The ensuing stillness is not the restful, peaceful kind, but is more like a void suddenly filled with embarrassment, surprise, and perhaps a touch of shame.

Reflection on the Scene

This incident is told differently in the original story. In the novel that the movie was based on, *Flowers for Algernon*, the author has Charly explode with anger and chastise the patrons for their cruelty. Actor Cliff Robertson, who played Charly and controlled the rights to the play, did not think that an outburst of anger was appropriate, as it would neither help the crowd understand their cruelty nor restore the boy's lost dignity. Instead, the actor wrote this more satisfying scene of spilled-glasses grace.

Charly's act of kindness speaks far more eloquently than do words, especially words of anger. Like Jesus in the synagogue, Charly reaches out to the unfortunate victim and shows by his assistance that he understands the pain of the person and seeks to restore his sense of worth. Although he *is* angry, his simple deed of kindness is all the rebuke that the patrons need in order to understand how inadequate their response to the boy's plight had been.

The plight of the just man described by the Psalmist is that of the busboy—and was once Charly's also. Too often the disabled are surrounded by people who "close their hearts to pity. . . . They track me down; now they surround me; they set their eyes to cast me to the ground." Both Charly at the bakery and the busboy at the restaurant have suffered from those "who close their hearts to pity." At such times even the simplest act of kindness is as welcome as a cloudburst to a parched traveler lost in the desert. In such moments of grace, we identify with the person in need.

When Jesus took the towel and basin of water and knelt down to wash the dirty feet of his disciples, he identified himself so with their need that he set aside his position of master to take the role of a slave. In that restaurant, Charly also set aside his newfound position of privilege to go to the side of and kneel down with one who needed desperately the affirmation that, despite his mistake and slowness of comprehension, he was a person of worth.

Even those who are not so afflicted feel this way at times when family, friends, or colleagues turn on them. At such moments when it seems that all have abandoned us, even the smallest act of kindness directed our way is welcome. At such times we know what grace is and how much each human being needs it, no matter how smart or slow.

For Further Reflection

1. How do you feel around a mentally or physically handicapped person? Embarrassed? Uncomfortable? Superior? Grateful ("There but for the grace of God go I")?

2. Have you been in the Psalmist's position? Or have you been part of a group that put down a Charly— perhaps when you were a child or teenager?

3. Have you felt as Jesus did around someone in need who was being neglected or abused by others? What did you do? Would you change anything if you could do it over again?

4. Which is more basic—feelings or intelligence? Why do you think that some people think they can insult or patronize a "slow" person?

5. What do you think of Cliff Robertson's rewrite of the scene? How is the simple act of "spilled-glass grace" more powerful than the novel's dramatic scene of righteous anger? What kind of impression might each make on the callous onlookers?

6. Does your neighborhood or church have a person like Charly, someone with a disability who would appreciate some attention from you?

HYMN: "The Light of God Is Falling"

A Prayer

O God, who speaks to us in such simple acts as washing feet or picking up spilled glasses, may we who have received so much of your grace also be channels of your gracious love. Make us more sensitive to those around us, especially those like Charly Gordon who are so vulnerable to our callous or unthinking words and acts. May we see in each new day opportunities to give and receive your tender mercies. We pray in the name of the One who loved and touched those scorned by the society of his day, Jesus Christ, our Lord. Amen.

3. Laundry-Room Grace
American History X

Note: Be cautious if using this with a group. The film includes strong street language and two scenes of wrenching violence, the latter including a prison rape scene. Therefore this should be used only when the group is mature and with advance warning given.

> Create in me a clean heart, O God,
>   and put a new and right spirit within me.
> Do not cast me away from your presence,
>   and do not take your holy spirit from me.
> Restore to me the joy of your salvation,
>   and sustain in me a willing spirit.
>
> Then I will teach transgressors your ways,
>   and sinners will return to you.
> Deliver me from bloodshed, O God,
>   O God of my salvation,
>   and my tongue will sing aloud of your
>   deliverance.
>
> Psalm 51:10–14

> From now on, therefore, we regard no one from a human point of view; even though we once knew Christ from a human point of view, we know him no longer in that way. So if anyone is in Christ, there is a new creation: everything old has passed away; see, everything has become new!
>
> 2 Corinthians 5:16–17

Introduction

Derek has been sentenced to a long prison term for stomping to death a young black man. The victim had been a member of a gang vandalizing his car late one night. Derek himself belonged to a gang of neo-Nazi skinheads backed by a shadowy older professional white supremacist. Derek was so into racial hatred that he had a large swastika tattooed across his chest. All the young skinheads looked to him for leadership; in fact, he had recruited many of them.

During Derek's time in the penitentiary, his younger brother Danny, who has always idolized him, follows in his brother's footsteps and joins the gang, imbibing its racist ideology. Throughout this time, Sweeney, the black school principal and civics teacher, tries to counteract the racism he sees poisoning the boy and sending him down the path chosen by Derek. Sweeney also has kept in touch with Derek and is helpful when Derek comes up for parole. When Danny turns in a paper on great leaders in which he blatantly praises Adolph Hitler, Sweeney orders the boy to write a new one. His assignment is to turn in a report on his brother, describing how he became a skinhead and then a convict. Danny resists the idea, but he wants to pass the class, so he agrees, giving the paper the title "American History X."

At this moment, Derek has returned home and sets out to extricate his brother from what he now perceives as an evil group. He tells Danny the story of what happened to him in prison. He had arrived there, arrogantly proclaiming his beliefs by his shaved head and swastika tattoo. The majority black population looked upon him with disdain, but the corps of skinheads welcomed him, seeing him as an addition to their ranks. However, the trial and prison sentence has sobered Derek. He decides to go it alone, declining to sit at mess with the neo-Nazis. He has had enough of trouble. This, of course, does not sit well with them. He is warned that attempting to go it alone could be dangerous in such a predatory place where the strong prey on the weak.

Sure enough, one day the skinheads corner Derek in the showers. While the paid-off guard looks the other way, the gang brutally rapes and beats him, leaving him prostrate on the wet floor. It is while he is recovering in the prison infirmary that Sweeney comes to him and offers to help. Derek neither tells who attacked him nor accepts the neo-Nazis' invitation to sit with them in the mess hall. They are angry at his refusal, giving Derek good cause to expect another attack.

The Scenes

Derek is assigned to work in the laundry room folding sheets and pillowcases. This is the best thing that could happen to him, because his workmate is Lamont. Lamont is a young African American who loves to talk and joke. Derek at first makes no response other than a nod or gesture. Lamont must know about the attack on Derek, and he certainly is aware of his workmate's racial/political views, so loudly proclaimed by the swastika tattoo. Nonetheless, Lamont keeps up his friendly patter each time they work together, showing Derek how to fold the bed linens, advising him another time to slow down and make the work last out the allotted time, and then, in a very serious vein, warning Derek that his decision to go it alone is a very danger-ous one. In prison, he declares, you need connections, you need someone to guard your back. By now Derek has warmed up to his friend and is responding. He laughs heartily at Lamont's story of his being arrested for assaulting an officer, claiming that he merely picked up the stolen TV set and then dropped it on the policeman's foot by accident when arrested.

Derek continues telling his story to Danny by admitting that he lived in great fear during his final weeks in prison, each day fearing a new attack from the skinheads. Especially as the date for his parole (Sweeney had vouched for him) draws near, Derek thinks his luck will run out. But the attack never comes. He walks toward the prison gate and sees Lamont. He thanks him, and when Lamont tells him there's nothing calling for this, Derek says that he thinks Lamont is the reason the skinheads never came for him. Lamont must have told his black friends, and they let the whites know there would be serious repercussions if Derek was harmed. Lamont still denies it, but Derek thanks him again and walks out the prison gate a free man.

Reflection on the Scene

Derek is free not just from the walls of the prison; he is free in a far deeper sense, thanks to the graciousness of an African American who refused to play a white man's racist game. Lamont knew that he had to get along with his new partner if their days were to be pleasant, so day after day he chipped away at the wall of Derek's racism with his stream of talk that was a mixture of humor, advice, and general observations. Through Lamont God has, in the words of the Psalmist, "created a clean heart" and "put a new and right spirit within" Derek. Day by day, through his good will Lamont has shown his racist friend that underneath the dark skin a black person could be kind and generous. Derek's racism had not allowed him to see this possibility.

What has happened to Derek is what Paul describes to the Corinthians as happening to those who are "in Christ." They become "new creations." "From now on, therefore, we regard no one from a human point of view; even though we once knew Christ from a human point of view, we know him no longer in that way." Derek no longer looks at his black friend from a human, or racist, view. Lamont is not just a "colored" or a "n—"; he is *Lamont*, fellow prisoner and workmate, the guy who helps out a buddy when he needs him.

Millions of white Americans have undergone an experience—we might call it a conversion—similar to Derek's. The circumstance has not been as dire, probably. Nonetheless, the transformation has been from regarding members of one group—be they blacks, Mexicans, Jews, or Italians—as inferior, to looking upon them as equals and maybe even as possible friends. Raised by prejudiced parents in a society that generally supported their prejudice, many of us who are white have felt challenged when we have encountered a member of the despised group for the first time—at school, work, or in the armed services (but seldom, it is sad to say, in our segregated church, the one place where all differences should have been overcome "in Christ"!). The process within us took time; years of embedded racism cannot be overcome in a day. Day-to-day contact was needed during which the persons who our prejudice taught us "always" acted in one way did not in fact do so. Sometimes we might have run away from such contact; the old system of segregation was designed to keep such contact to a minimum. In Derek's case this was not possible, and so the Christ, working through Lamont, slowly tore down "the dividing wall of hostility," as the apostle Paul put it in another of his letters.

Derek entered the prison enslaved to prejudice and hatred. He left it freed to engage in what Paul called "the ministry of reconciliation," which in his case was to bring his brother Danny into the same freedom from hostility and racism.

For Further Reflection

1. How has racism affected you and your life? What racial beliefs did your parents pass on to you? Have you had to correct some of the stories and stereotypes? How did your childhood friends view those of different racial and ethnic backgrounds?

2. When you hear the following, what images come to mind? Are they positive or negative?

- Blacks
- Jews
- Mexican/Hispanic
- Italian
- Whites
- Gypsy
- Indian
- Homosexual
- Mentally handicapped/Retarded
- Cripple
- Blind

3. Where do we get such images and labels? In the film, there is a flashback scene in which we see the boys' deceased father filling their minds with his racist views in regard to affirmative action and the capabilities of African Americans. (If you are using this guide in a group, you might play the Rogers and Hammerstein

song from *South Pacific* "You've Got to Be Taught" at this point.) How did the circumstances of the father's death reinforce this teaching? Is not part of the difficulty of stereotypes the fact that there is a kernel of truth around which generalizations are falsely woven?

4. Lamont is clearly an agent of grace in the story. What might have happened to him to prevent the bitterness that often arises in the hearts of victims of oppression? Do you find such bitterness among minority members of your community? How is this also a fruit of racism?

5. How did you leave behind what the apostle Paul called a "human point of view" of racial-ethnic groups other than your own? (Note that I do not say "racism," which will always remain within us, though its power is diminished and eventually broken by our transformation.) Did your faith or the church help? Or was it more through frequent, and positive, contact with minority members?

6. What is your church doing to increase the contact between different groups? There are many programs designed to break down the walls of racism. Where do you see them being put into place in your community? Think and pray about how you can become a part of such efforts to work with God in building what Dr. Martin Luther King Jr. called "the Beloved Community."

HYMN: "In Christ There Is No East or West"

A Prayer

Gracious and loving God, how you must weep at times to see how your children treat one another: Irish killing

Irish because of a difference in religion; Serbs and Muslims, Palestinians and Jews killing each other; and in our own country, frequent displays of hatred between whites and blacks. Cleanse me of all forms of prejudice by renewing my heart and instilling in my mind a new vision of how you want us to live together. Lead me to those places in my church and community where others are working to tear down the old dividing walls of hostility, so that I might join them. I thank you that you are at work in bringing about reconciliation through such films as this one. May you bless those who made it and those who watch it. We ask this through Jesus Christ, brother to all who believe. Amen.

4. Truthful Grace
Saturday Night Fever

Whenever you possibly can, do good to those who need it.

Proverbs 3:27 (TEV)

You will know the truth, and the truth will make you free.

John 8:32

God presides in the heavenly council;
  in the assembly of the gods he gives his
    decision:
"You must stop judging unjustly;
  you must no longer be partial to the wicked!
Defend the rights of the poor and the orphans;
  be fair to the needy and the helpless.
Rescue them from the power of evil men."

Psalm 82:1–4 (TEV)

Introduction

Nineteen-year-old Tony Manero works hard during the week at a Brooklyn hardware/paint store stocking materials and waiting on customers. His work routine is dull and drab, with little to stir or stimulate his imagination. He lives for weekends. It is only then that Tony comes alive, shedding his usual clothes to don a flowered shirt and a beautiful white suit that declare how special their owner is, especially on the dance-hall floor, where Tony fairly sparkles. At the popular 2000 Odyssey Club, where Saturday night fever takes hold of those on the dance floor, Tony *is* special. He is regarded by virtually everyone there as the best dancer, blessed with a lithe body and all the right moves. On Saturday nights he and his gyrating friends can forget their workaday existence as they respond to the driving beat of the disco songs.

The disco scene is almost a religion for Tony and his friends. His parents try to discourage him from attending each Saturday evening as Tony primps and changes from his everyday clothes into his white disco suit. Regarding the dance scene as frivolous at best, and sin producing at worst, they compare him to his serious brother, Frank. His older brother is studying for the priesthood, so in such a staunchly Roman Catholic family the comparison between Tony and Frank is far from favorable. What the parents do not realize is that Frank is troubled concerning his own vocation as a priest. During their family talks, Frank is nonjudgmental, and yet questions are raised in Tony's mind about the direction of his own future.

One night Tony meets Stephanie. She is somewhat older than he, but she is strikingly beautiful—and equally important to Tony, she is a fine dancer. The two agree to pair up. There is a dance contest coming up at which the winners will be crowned the king and queen of the disco club. This will confirm what Tony and his friends believe—that he rules the floor of Odyssey 2000. Tony and Stephanie practice hard. There are a number of complications before the big night arrives, but finally on the night of the event Tony and Stephanie are ready. They are convinced that their hours of hard work at getting their steps and moves perfect will be rewarded.

The Scene

The dance hall is crowded with contestants and onlookers. When it comes time for Stephanie and Tony to dance, they give it their all. They perform their steps and moves to perfection before the gaze of the admiring audience. Tony has forgotten all family disapproval and other problems. Saturday night fever bans all other cares or thoughts. Tony focuses his attention totally upon the moment when every move of the feet and arms, every undulation of their bodies is being taken in by the audience. Their number comes to an end, and the two walk off the floor to a loud ovation. Tony is certain that the crown is theirs.

But then another couple takes to the floor. The audience is not pleased by their dark skin. They are Puerto Rican, and Odyssey 2000 is patronized mostly by young adults of Italian descent. The music begins, and the couple move gracefully across the floor. Tony watches them at first with only half interest, his mind being occupied by the many compliments his admirers shower upon him. Then, as the Puerto Ricans' performance increases in tempo and daring moves, he turns his attention back to the dance floor, and his admiration grows. They are good, he admits, very good. He knows that he and Stephanie had done well, but his confidence that they deserve the crown is shaken.

The music stops, but the audience, blinded by their prejudice, fails to reward the couple with applause. Even more, when the MC calls for the audience to vote, the crowd gives the award to Tony and Stephanie. By now Tony has faced the truth that the Puerto Rican couple performed better than he and his partner did. He and Stephanie are called up and given the trophy cup. However, instead of parading around with it in triumph, Tony walks over to the ones he knows are the true victors. To the astonishment of all, he hands the trophy to the Puerto Rican couple and walks out of the hall for the last time.

Reflection on the Scene

In the last scene we know that Tony's act of truthful grace is the turning point of his life. All through the film he has wanted to leave his drab existence. He has thought that the world of disco dancing would provide him the freedom he longed for. But now he knows that it is a world built upon illusion. The refusal of the crowd to award the prize to the true winners made him aware of this for the first time. Thus Tony leaves not only the hall but Brooklyn itself behind as he walks across the Brooklyn Bridge toward the sparkling lights of Manhattan. He at last has made the break from his past life. His new one might also be full of illusion, Manhattan itself being full of people striving after the wind; but we can hope that Tony's new maturity will stand him in good stead.

Saturday Night Fever deals well with themes of prejudice, integrity, and coming to the truth, as well as with the American obsession for winning. Tony and Stephanie are superb dancers, and they perform well at the contest. But the Puerto Rican couple who follow them do even better, and Tony knows this. He also is aware of the hostility of his prejudiced supporters. When he received the coveted trophy, he could have swept aside his knowledge of the situation and basked in the admiration of the crowd. But Tony is like what some would call a "righteous Gentile," one who does the law of God without being fully aware of it. He is aware that an injustice has been done, and he sets forth with the trophy to right the wrong by giving the trophy to those who truly deserve it. As an artist, Tony cannot live with a lie. His giving over the prize is a rebuke to those who awarded it unjustly to him. Whether the crowd will realize that they have committed a wrong is immaterial to Tony. *He* knows, and this is enough. His act of truthful grace has set him free. He might not see Christ in his act, but the Savior's words surely apply to him at this turning point in his life: "You will know the truth, and the truth will make you free."

Our growth toward maturity could be described in terms of the shedding or stripping away of the lies and illusions that enslave us. For Tony, it was the facing up to the truth of his friends' prejudice and the fact that his disco world was not real. For us the facing up to a truth will be different because of our circumstances. We might not live in Brooklyn or be surrounded by friends who look down on particular ethnic groups, and we might possess two left feet that bar us from graceful dance moves. Nonetheless, illusions of race and pride, of what is real and what is false, abound. We too must come to know the truth that will make us free. For Christians, this truth is found in the life and teachings of the One who first said those words.

For Further Reflection

1. If you watched the film, were you surprised when Tony gave the trophy to the Puerto Rican couple? How does this act confirm the definition of grace as an unexpected gift (but not, in this case, of "unmerited," for the other team in Tony's eyes deserved the prize)?

2. What similar acts of "truthful grace" have you heard or read about? We read in our newspapers of robberies and embezzlements every day. How often do we see stories of people turning in wallets filled with money, or customers telling a cashier that too much change was given? A student telling a teacher that she was given a higher grade than she deserved? A tennis player admitting that a ball was not out-of-bounds on his side, as the referee and opponent had thought?

3. What similar instances of bias have you seen? From referees at sports events? Preferences in choosing leaders at clubs, church, or work? Was there anything you could do about it, and if so, did you?

4. When you do not act to correct a known wrong, how do you feel about yourself? What acts of grace in your relationship with others do you still need to perform? What truths do you need to face up to? How can your faith in Christ aid in this?

HYMN: "Be Thou My Vision"

A Prayer

Gracious and loving Father, we thank you for those who serve as examples of courage and integrity, who face up to the truth in their lives and then walk away from lies and illusions that would enslave them. Help us courageously to see our own lives, to sort out truth from fiction, and to receive the strength to live by the truth. Give us your Holy Spirit so that we who profess faith in Christ "will know the truth, and the truth will make us free." Amen.

5. Grace in Suffering
Marvin's Room

How very good and pleasant it is
    when kindred live together in unity!
It is like the precious oil on the head,
    running down upon the beard,
on the beard of Aaron,
    running down over the collar of his robes.
It is like the dew of Hermon,
    which falls on the mountains of Zion.
For there the LORD ordained his blessing,
    life forevermore.

Psalm 133

James and John, the sons of Zebedee, came forward to him, and said to him, "Teacher, we want you to do for us whatever we ask of you. . . . Grant us to sit, one at your right hand and one at your left, in your glory." But Jesus said to them, "You do not know what you are asking. . . . [W]hoever would be great among you must be your servant. . . . For the Son of man also came not to be served but to serve, and to give his life as a ransom for many."

Mark 10:35–45 (RSV)

Introduction

Bessie and Lee are sisters who have communicated little with one another over the years. Bessie gave up her personal plans and returned to Florida when their father, Marvin, came down with a debilitating illness. Rather than place him in a home, Bessie has cared for him and his eccentric sister over the years, Marvin's room becoming the center of her existence. Lee, always cherishing her independence, has left home never to look back. Married and then abandoned by her husband, she has raised her son, Hank, by herself, but not with great success. The troubled teenager is always at war with her and with himself, his raging anger expressed by setting off fires. The latest is to their own house, so Lee has sent him to a mental institution for treatment. Lee's greatest accomplishment, in her eyes, is a newly won degree in cosmetology, which she hopes will help her to open her own beauty shop. But when Bessie calls asking for help, Lee takes her son out of the hospital and heads for Florida.

Bessie has been diagnosed as having leukemia. The hope is that either Lee or Hank might have bone marrow that matches hers. Old hurts and slights open up as the three are united, Hank especially being resentful of his aunt's long neglect of him and his mother. But Bessie is able eventually to regain Hank's trust and the love of her sister. Near the end of the film, Bessie and Lee stand in their father's room and share their deep feelings and dreams.

The Scene

Bessie and Lee talk about the different paths they have taken—Lee seeking her life away from the family, and

Bessie giving up her own plans to care for her father and aunt. Bessie says she has no regrets for following her path. "I have been wonderfully blessed with love," she declares. Lee understandably thinks that her sister is speaking of the love and gratitude from their father and aunt for all her years of sacrifice. No, Bessie corrects her. She is blessed by having the opportunity to *give* so much love to them!

Reflection on the Scene

Many families become divided over the years, some members drifting away and seldom contacting one another. Like Lee, they might want to achieve their own goals and be unencumbered by family obligations. Like Bessie, those who remain in the hometown often become so preoccupied with responsibilities that they fail to make the effort to keep in touch. The film encourages an optimistic hope that during a crisis estranged family members can come together and overcome their differences for the good of all. Then they discover what the Psalmist meant by his declaration, "How very good and pleasant it is when kindred live together in unity!"

Some, however, have found the film and the play it is based on too optimistic. One person who had given long-term care to an ailing parent wrote that she could not agree with Bessie's observation about being blessed. Her experience was of one long period of hellish tending to cleaning odorous wounds, soiled sheets, and bedpans. Little of the day-to-day misery of caring for the chronically ill is shown in the film. Nor does the film, like so many Hollywood productions, indicate that Bessie had much of a spiritual or religious life. Most people involved in a church not only would have recourse to prayer and public worship, but also would receive visits by the pastor and other church members. They would be the object of intercessory prayers and the offer of meals and volunteers willing to give the caretaker occasional breaks to get out and shop or just enjoy life. Maybe we can assume all this in Bessie's case. What we do see is that she has learned the secret of living taught by Christ when his status- and power-seeking disciples came to him with their request that they be allowed the special seats beside him in the kingdom of God. Jesus pointedly replied that only those who learn to serve will rule, even as he "came not to be served but to serve." Bessie is a good example of what Jesus meant.

For Further Reflection

1. Does the film make you think of relationships in your own family? Is there someone like Bessie in your family to whom the others look for leadership and special care during a crisis? Is there someone like Lee, who always seems to want to do her own thing? Do you identify more with Lee or with Bessie?

2. What has happened during crises in your family? Have the family members come together and been able to settle differences so that they "pull together" to help whoever is in need? Or has the crisis brought to the surface long-simmering resentments and memories of past slights?

3. Can you recall times when, like Bessie, you received a blessing from some illness or difficulty? What was it that enabled you to see some light where others might see only darkness? Your faith? Spiritual practices such as prayer, reading, and meditating?

Conversation with and support of friends and other family members? Your church?

4. What has been your experience of Jesus' observation about serving versus being served? Are those who struggle to get ahead at almost any cost really happy or enjoyable to be around? Think about or discuss this observation: When an airliner arrives at its destination, many passengers hastily unsnap their safety belts, scramble to their feet, and grab their carry-on baggage from the overhead compartment so they can be first off the plane. But they must stand in the aisle for at least five minutes until the door is opened and the first-class passengers disembark. Others, however, sit back and continue to read or relax until the hustlers have scurried off. Who makes the best use of that time?

5. Think through a list of your friends and family. Who seems to be the happiest—those who are the wealthiest or those actively involved in serving others? Whom do you enjoy being around the most? Do others seem to like being around you? If not, what can you do to be more welcoming and spiritually attractive?

HYMN: "Christ of the Upward Way"

A Prayer

Gracious and loving God, we thank you that you are always with us in the midst of the joys and the sorrows of life. We do not always see you during our times of crises because we have allowed our tears of self-pity to cloud or blind our vision. Yet at other times we have experienced the joy that you bring, even in the midst of pain and sorrow, and we have discovered that such times bring us the opportunity to give love as well as to receive it. Continue to help us by your Spirit in the ongoing struggle between our desires to serve and to be served. Deepen our commitment to the One who lived and died by the principle that "it is more blessed to give than to receive." This we ask in his holy name, Jesus Christ, our Lord. Amen.

6. By His Stripes
Empire of the Sun

But he was wounded for our transgressions,
    crushed for our iniquities;
upon him was the punishment that made us whole,
    and by his bruises we are healed.

Isaiah 53:5

Then Pilate took Jesus and had him flogged. And the soldiers wove a crown of thorns and put it on his head, and they dressed him in a purple robe. They kept coming up to him, saying, "Hail, King of the Jews!" and striking him on the face. Pilate went out again and said to them, "Look, I am bringing him out to you to let you know that I find no case against him." So, Jesus came out, wearing the crown of thorns and the purple robe. Pilate said to them, "Here is the man!"

John 19:1–5

Bless those who persecute you; bless and do not curse them. . . . Beloved, never avenge yourselves, but leave room for the wrath of God. . . . No, "if your enemies are hungry, feed them; if they are thirsty, give them something to drink; for by doing this you will heap burning coals on their heads." Do not be overcome by evil, but overcome evil with good.

Romans 12:14–21

Introduction

Young Jim Graham, fascinated by the Japanese and their war planes, is separated from his parents during the evacuation of Shanghai at the beginning of the Second World War. After a series of adventures during which he almost starves, he is interred in a Japanese prison camp, where his energy and ingenuity earn him a place of honor and respect in the eyes of many of the British and American prisoners. Toward the end of the war, American bombers fly over the Shanghai waterfront one night, their bombs starting great fires as they score hits on the docks and warehouses. Jim, realizing that the vindictive camp Commander will probably vent his rage on the helpless, ill patients, rushes to reach the camp infirmary ahead of the raging Japanese.

The Scene

At the prison infirmary, the doctor sees the angry Commander and his staff striding toward him. He orders the nurses inside to move the patients away from the windows. The Commander, a staff in hand, starts to go through the door to the hospital, but the doctor blocks his way. This inflames the Commander even more. He knocks the doctor down and starts to beat him. It is then that Jim enters the crowded, tense scene.

To divert the Commander, Jim yells his name, at the same time smashing a window. Then he goes to the Commander and falls on the floor before him. The Japanese soldier stops his shouting, startled at what he sees—Jim has bared his back to him. The boy is ready to take the blows meant for the doctor. There is a pause, the atmosphere tense, with all the guards and prisoners watching in total silence to see what the

Commander will do. After a suspenseful moment, the officer turns on his heel and strides back toward his own quarters, his aides following him. The doctor and Jim are left with no further harm.

Reflection on the Scene

Young Jim is an unlikely candidate to be a carrier of grace. He has learned from his cruel American mentor survival tactics in the harsh environment of the prison camp, a place where only the strong will get enough to eat, and only those who get enough to eat will survive illness and brutality. Yet something of his training at an Anglican school has remained intact, for in several instances Jim helps others, sometimes at risk to himself. This is especially true in this incident when he offers his back to the hard staff of the Japanese officer. The man backs down, but Jim could not foresee this. He was willing to receive the blows in place of his friend the doctor, because he apparently believed that his friend was vital to the well-being of the camp. Jim's self-sacrifice thus becomes an inspiration to all, even as the greater sacrifice of Jesus continues to awe us. Jim was more fortunate, of course, than Jesus, in that Jim's enemy saw and responded to the goodness of his act. Pilate did recognize the goodness (or innocence) of his prisoner, but Pilate was weaker than the religious leaders and their mob, so he caved in to their threats and went along with their murderous intent.

It is doubtful that Jim, at his young age, had heard of another prisoner being held at the same time in a British prison in India, but Jim's deed would have received the wholehearted approval of Mohandas Gandhi. The great leader seeking Indian independence from Jim's own country taught that such unorthodox acts as Jim's were the best way to confront an enemy. Jim at the time would have seen his as an act of the weak and the powerless, but Gandhi taught that only the really strong of heart, mind, and spirit could defy the powerful and take the consequences. It would be too much to assume that Jim bared his back out of love, especially a love for the Japanese commander, but Jim is not far from this. Like the One who taught the ethic of turning the other cheek, Jim is not far from the kingdom of heaven.

For Further Reflection

1. Who in your experience has made this kind of sacrifice for others? Was it for you? How did you feel about this?

2. Is this the kind of sacrifice parents are frequently asked to make for the good of their children?

3. What is the reaction to others of such sacrifice? How is Jim's act similar to Jesus' commandment to "turn the other cheek"? Could you do this? What would aid you in following his command?

4. Jesus tells his followers that they too must take up their cross and follow him. Where is the cross in your past and present experience? Where do you find the strength and will to do this?

5. Do you think that baring the back out of love would have more impact than baring it out of duty? What is the difference? Which is also concerned about the welfare of the enemy as well as friends and oneself? The apostle Paul quotes from Proverbs approvingly when he advises his readers at Rome to look out for the welfare of their enemies. What do you think he means

that treating the enemy well "will heap burning coals on their heads"? Do you think this is what happened in the case of the Japanese commander? What kind of a world might you help create if you dealt this way with those who consider you as their enemy?

HYMN: "When I Survey the Wondrous Cross" or "O Master, Let Me Walk with Thee"

A Prayer

Dear God, we thank you that your Son was willing to live out the ancient prophecy of one who would bare his back to his enemies on behalf of us all. Because of his sacrifice we see how much you love us. Help us to live in such similar ways that our own sacrifices will be a blessing to others. Help us to rise above our culture of comfort and self-indulgence so that we can walk the way of the cross, always with the knowledge that Christ walks with us. We ask this in his name. Amen.

7. Dirty-Feet Grace
Entertaining Angels: The Dorothy Day Story

Happy are those who consider the poor,
    the LORD delivers them in the day of trouble.
                              Psalm 41:1

[Jesus said to them,] "Do you know what I have done to you? You call me Teacher and Lord—and you are right, for that is what I am. So if I, your Lord and Teacher, have washed your feet, you also ought to wash one another's feet. For I have set you an example, that you also should do as I have done to you. Very truly, I tell you, servants are not greater than their master, nor are messengers greater than the one who sent them."

John 13:12b–17

Let each of you look not to your own interests, but to the interests of others. Let the same mind be in you that was in Christ Jesus,
> who, though he was in the form of God,
> > did not regard equality with God
> > as something to be exploited,
> but emptied himself,
> > taking the form of a slave,
> > being born in human likeness.
> And being found in human form,
> > he humbled himself
> > and became obedient to the point of death—
> > even death on a cross.

Philippians 2:4–8

Introduction

Entertaining Angels: The Dorothy Day Story presents us with the story of the early life of one of the great Christian social activists of the twentieth century. Once a journalist for a communist newspaper and the consort of various Greenwich Village radicals, Dorothy was converted to Christ, partly because of the birth of her daughter and partly through contact with a Roman Catholic nun who was working with and feeding the poor. Dorothy had earlier expressed an emptiness in her life and confusion as to what she should do with her life. Peter Maurin, a French lay Roman Catholic, came to New York to work with the poor. He read some of Dorothy's passionately written newspaper articles about the plight of the oppressed.

Sensing her empathy for the downtrodden, he attached himself to her, becoming her mentor in theology and social ethics, convincing her to risk her meager savings on the founding of a newspaper, *The Catholic Worker*, which was dedicated to serving those at the bottom of society.

Challenged by Peter, Dorothy began to take in homeless people. Her little apartment shared with her brother and sister-in-law became too crowded, so she rented a storefront to serve as both the offices for her newspaper and as a safe place for the street people to stay in. When he was not staying with her, Peter Maurin often slept in the streets with the people whom he was trying to help in the name of Christ. In the following scene, we see how Peter Maurin was like Christ and St. Francis.

The Scene

Photographed in warm colors, this night scene looks as if it could have been painted by Caravaggio or Rembrandt. An elderly, raggedly dressed man sits on the floor of the Worker's House, his back resting against the wall. Peter kneels beside the man and gently removes the remnants of the man's shoes. They are literally falling apart. His feet are bloody, with pus oozing out of numerous wounds. With a basin of water and a rag, Peter gently washes the exhausted man's feet. Dorothy watches them. As Peter dries the man's feet, he notices again the terrible condition of the man's shoes. Peter removes his own shoes and places them on the man's feet. The astonished Dorothy asks Peter what he is going to do about shoes for himself. Peter does not answer. His own feet are the furthest thing from his mind during this touching moment of grace.

Reflection on the Scene

As John declares in his Gospel account, Jesus washed the feet of his disciples as an example of the servanthood he expected them to imitate. Luke, in his account, relates that the Twelve, even in the Upper Room, had been arguing among themselves about who would be the greatest in their Master's kingdom. In his gentle rebuke Jesus says, "But I am among you as one who serves" (Luke 22:27). John shows us this as an acted-out parable. No doubt this inspired both Peter Maurin and the filmmakers, who chose to depict the scene like one of the paintings of an old master.

In turn, Peter challenges us to take up lowly tasks with little or no rewards. Every church, organization, or office has tasks that no one wants, from cleaning up after others to contacting people and asking them to take on difficult assignments. A friend told me once that many years ago he had gone to hear the great Japanese theologian Kagawa. Afterward my friend went to use the men's room. A number of conference participants were filing out the door. Many of them had missed the waste receptacle when they discarded their paper towels. He saw a small man stooping down, gathering up the paper, and placing it into the container. When the man looked up at him, my friend recognized that it was Kagawa. Kagawa and Peter, like Christ, show us that it is in tending to such lowly tasks that true discipleship is exercised. When confronted with a fellow human being with tired feet and torn-up shoes, Peter seems to ask us, "What else can I do but what I did?"

For Further Reflection

1. What jobs do you dislike the most? Jobs in your home, at church, at your place of work, in your social

life? How can doing these faithfully and competently be a measure of discipleship?

2. What great or showy positions of responsibility would you like to be asked to take up? Are these positions really more important in the eyes of your colleagues? In the eyes of Christ or Peter? How is what Peter Maurin did an act of "emptying himself"? Is this why he does not think of the consequences of giving his shoes away?

3. Compare Peter's humble act to that of celebrities who insist on preferential treatment and luxurious accommodations (including some famous Christian entertainers) when they perform. Or compare it to the need for institutions and charities to promise bronze plaques with the names of donors attached to a hall or statue. How is the phrase "full of herself (himself)" an apt one? When one is full of oneself, is there any room left for Christ or neighbor?

4. For further inspiration, read again John 13. Also, if you have a copy, read the great scene early in Victor Hugo's novel *Les Misérables*, often called "The Bishop's Candlesticks." (See Meditation 1.)

5. What persons in your experience "emptied themselves" in serving others? Think of some specific examples. How are they "happy" in the way the Psalmist means? Have you felt this way at times?

HYMN: "O Master, Let Me Walk with Thee" or "Let There Be Light, Lord God of Hosts"

A Prayer

Dear God, you sent your Son from heaven to take up our human form—not that of a king or priest, but that of a lowly peasant. Though Jesus was tempted in the wilderness to use his wonderful powers to win greatness and glory, he chose the way of a servant instead, even taking up the lowly task of washing the feet of his friends. Help us also to stand against the temptations to seek power and greatness—the easy approval from peers who would puff up our pride and sense of self-worth until we are unable even to see the feet of friends, let alone stoop down to wash them. Give to us in those moments of quiet, unnoticed, and unacclaimed service that sense of joy in knowing that we are doing your will. This we ask in the name of the Great King who knelt to wash the dusty feet of others. Amen.

8. Grace to "See"
Smoke

The wise have eyes in their head,
  but fools walk in darkness.

Ecclesiastes 2:14

"Do you have eyes, and fail to see? Do you have ears, and fail to hear?"

Mark 8:18

Introduction

The action of Wayne Wang's sensitive film takes place in the politically incorrect environs of Auggie Wren's tobacco shop in Brooklyn. Paul Benjamin, a writer unable to write because he is still traumatized by the death of his wife, stops in almost every day. So had his wife, just a few moments before she was cut down in the cross fire between two gunmen. Paul and Auggie often chat, but it is always small talk until the evening that Paul notices Auggie's camera. Auggie is locking up the shop for the night when Paul rushes up and asks if he can still buy some smokes.

The Scene

As Auggie gets change, Paul notices the camera on the counter. Auggie reveals that he uses it every day. "So," Paul observes, "you're not just a guy pushing coins across a counter." Auggie, replying that that's all some people see, shows Paul his large photo album and invites him to look through it. Paul is somewhat surprised, amused, and bemused to see that all of the pictures were taken from Auggie's corner—pictures of people and cars passing by. They were taken from the same spot at the same time every day—8 A.M.! When Paul comments that this seems a bit strange, Auggie responds, "It's my corner. Just a small part of the world, but things happen here, too." Smiling at the eccentricity of it all, Paul flips through the pages, glancing from picture to picture. "Slow down," Auggie tells him. "You'll never get it unless you slow down, my friend." Paul does. He begins to notice the changes—in people, in shadows and lighting. He even spots his wife in one or two, passing by on her way to work. Tears form in his eyes. Auggie watches in silence, and as Paul cries and talks about his beloved wife, Auggie gently touches the writer's shoulder as a sign of his sympathy.

Reflection on the Scene

Every time I see this scene, the strains of Simon and Garfunkel's "59th Street Bridge Song" waft through my mind, with its admonition to slow down and not move so fast. We need our Auggies and songwriters to slow us down so that we will look around and observe how wonderful the world is that we pass through, and by, so quickly. When I was a boy in Indianapolis, the proprietor of my favorite bookstore was an artist who loved to leave the city to paint country scenes, especially of southern Indiana hills. One time a motorist stopped to ask what he was doing. "I'm painting the scenery," Mr. Erfurt replied. "What scenery?" the man asked, and then sped away before the astonished artist could reply. "What can you do with such a person?" Mr. Erfurt would say, throwing up his hands in mock despair. Let us hope that that unseeing motorist finally met his Auggie to open his eyes to all that he was missing.

I remember being a bit amused the first time I learned that the great artist Claude Monet had made twenty-six paintings of the facade of the Cathedral at Rouen. Why would someone want to paint the same scene more than a couple of times? Monet, of course, saw what I and most of his countrymen missed—how the facade appears so different at various times of the day when the sun strikes it from different angles, and on cloudy or rainy days when a mist obscures part of it. From his beautiful paintings you are made more aware of the daily marvel and beauty of the play of light upon an object. Monet's paintings help us all to slow down and see the exquisite in the ordinary.

Paul's encounter with Auggie is brief, but it has far-reaching ramifications. He sees Auggie in a new light—not just as a guy selling him cigars and "pushing coins across a counter," but as a perceptive human being, an artist with a camera. And through Auggie's camera (which later figures in the climactic story that helps Paul return to his writing), Paul sees the world in a different light. He begins to come out of his trance-like state and return to the world of people and relationships. He and Auggie become friends, and in a series of encounters, each becomes a channel of grace to another person who enters their lives.

For Further Reflection

1. If you plan to use this meditation with a group, look up a copy of the song "Everything Is Beautiful" and have it playing as the group assembles. Call attention to the line in which it is declared that no one is as blind as one who refuses to see.

2. Do you find it ironic that Paul, a writer, should be aided in "seeing" by a cigar store proprietor? After all, writers are supposed to help the rest of us perceive things more clearly and deeply. Is there an unlikely person in your past who helped you in an unexpected but significant way? Usually we feel indebted to a teacher or other such mentoring person, but was there someone else?

3. Jesus was upset that his hungry disciples, who had witnessed his miracle of feeding the multitudes, still did not perceive that he could meet their need. So he accused them of having eyes and ears but failing to see or hear. Where in your life might this charge be true for you? How has Christ become significant in fulfilling the deep hunger within yourself?

4. Are there people and circumstances that have escaped your notice because you have been moving too fast or had the sound of a radio or TV turned up too high? When are the times in your day when you can stop and think and pray?

5. We hear and read that there is a great hunger for spirituality in our fast-paced society. Although Auggie does not speak in terms generally recognized as spiritual, in what ways is he a very spiritual person? How do the special-effects appearances of God in "religious" movies (I'm thinking of the Cecil B. DeMille kind that raid the Bible for exciting stories) dull us to encounters with God in the midst of the ordinary, everyday world?

6. Think of one or two people whom you think of as rather unexciting or ordinary. Try an experiment of approaching them with fresh eyes. What might you have overlooked before because you did not really listen to them or notice any details of their clothing or possessions?

7. Read a classic devotional work such as Brother Lawrence's *The Practice of the Presence of God* to gain more insights into encountering God around your home or neighborhood, and not just in the formal liturgy of the church.

HYMN: "Day by Day" or "Open My Eyes that I Might See"

A Prayer

Dear God, you have given us eyes, but we do not always see; ears, but we do not always hear. Stir us by your Holy Spirit that we might see the world, especially its people, through your eyes, eyes of compassionate love and concern. Help us to slow down, look around, and see what a wonderful world you have created and what beautiful people you have given us to relate to. This we ask in the name of your Son, Jesus Christ, our Lord, who always seemed to have the time to stop and listen and converse with the least of your creation. Amen.

9. Love that Won't Go Away
The Great Santini

Bless the LORD, O my soul,
    and all that is within me,
    bless his holy name,
Bless the LORD, O my soul,
    and do not forget all his benefits—
who forgives all your iniquity,
    who heals all your diseases,
who redeems your life from the Pit,
    who crowns you with steadfast love and mercy,
who satisfies you with good as long as you live
    so that your youth is renewed like the eagle's.

Psalm 103:1–5

Two others also, who were criminals, were led away to be put to death with him. When they came to the place that is called The Skull, they crucified Jesus there with the criminals, one on his right and one on his left. Then Jesus said, "Father, forgive them; for they do not know what they are doing."

Luke 23:32–34a

For the message about the cross is foolishness to those who are perishing, but to us who are being saved it is the power of God.

1 Corinthians 1:18

Introduction

The Meechum family is *not* straight out of "Leave It to Beaver." "Bull" Meechum is a hotshot Marine pilot frustrated by a lack of action during the relatively peaceful late 1950s and early 1960s. He takes out his frustration on his family as he attempts to rule his wife, Lillian, and four children as if they were part of his air squadron. Lillian acts as a buffer, protecting the children and instilling in them gentler virtues. Ben, approaching his eighteenth birthday, is the most rebellious of the four. An excellent basketball player, he has a series of confrontations with Bull. Each time, Lillian tries to help Ben understand the seemingly cruel and irrational acts of his father. Late one night, the conflict almost comes to physical blows when Ben disobeys Bull's direct order not to go to the aid of his African-American friend Toomer, who was being attacked by a gang of racist toughs. Ben, taking his father's car, arrives too late to help his friend; during a struggle with his attackers, the black youth is accidentally shot by the gang leader. Ben helps his friend into the car and heads for the hospital. At the end of the lane, he comes upon his father, waving him down. Bull, angry at what he regards as his son's insubordination, berates Ben, but backs down when he looks in the car and discovers that Toomer is dying from his wounds.

The Scenes

Later that night, a drunken Bull and Lillian angrily shout at each other, and we hear a crashing sound. The four children rush downstairs to find Bull hitting their mother. They all jump on their father. This startles Bull. He pauses, especially taken aback by his tearful youngest son clinging to his leg and hitting at him. Bull breaks away and staggers out the door into the darkness. Lillian calms the children and sends the younger three to bed. Ben angrily comments that he hopes his father dies out there in the darkness. Lillian hushes him, expressing her worry that Bull will be discovered on base in his drunken state, thereby ending his already shaky military career. She asks Ben to go and find him. When he refuses, she orders him to go.

Ben calls for his dad in the dark, deserted streets. Hearing a voice and the crash of a bottle breaking, he heads for a large tree, where his father sits muttering out loud to an imaginary Lillian. "No, no Lil, you just don't understand. You gentle him too much. Too much. He won't make it. Meechum, Terror of the Skies! Father, Daddy, Poppa. You guys! Lil, you kids, I'll tell you what. You do the caring for me. Deal? Deal!" He cries softly. Ben stands mutely, listening to his father pour his heart out for the first time. "Poppa, Poppa. Ben! Watch out! You gotta be fast, cause the bogeys will get you. Defense, defense! You gotta work that defense, Benny. You gotta watch your six! Now you guard me. Lilly!"

Ben calls to him, "Dad." "I'm sick, boy," Bull answers. He coughs up something and then looks around. "Come on," Ben says, "Let's go home. Dad, let's go home, you and me." Bull, getting up, leans on Ben. "Dad, I think I understand now. Dad—I love you, Dad!" This is too much for the tough pilot. He breaks away, staggers, and Ben continues, "Did you hear what I said? I love you! Did you hear me? Did you hear me, Santini?" Ben dances around his woozy father, who tries to punch him. He fails to connect. "Watch your six, now! Guard me, guard me! I love you, Dad!" His father swings at him again. "Who-o-a-a! I love you! And there's nothing you can do about it!" They both fall to the ground. Ben, helping his father up, says, "Come on, let's go home."

Reflection on the Scene

The loyal love of Lillian, so much like that which Christ exhibited on the cross to his enemies, breaks through the smoldering hostility of her son. Like the shepherd going out after a lost sheep, Ben sets out to find his father. Upon finding him, he finally begins to understand why Bull has been so tough on him. Ben realizes that the emotionally inadequate Bull had turned over the job of nurturing the children to Lillian while he assumed the macho role of earning the money and defending the family in what he regarded as a very hostile world. In an instant Ben realizes that the love shown by his mother was the only medicine that could heal the sick soul of his father. In an outpouring of love that must have caused the angels of heaven to sing for joy, Ben storms the hostile defenses of his father, overcoming his resistance. It is one of the most beautiful moments in cinema, one that should nurture and inspire us to do likewise when we find ourselves in a situation of familial suspicion and hostility. Ben and Bull, like the Psalmist, have experienced the mercy of a loving God, in their case mediated through the patient suffering of a devoted wife and mother.

For Further Reflection

1. What kind of love does it take for Lillian to send her son out after the husband who just hit her? Some have angrily reacted to her act, branding her an "enabler." What do you think? Is such love sometimes "foolish," the kind of "foolishness" the apostle Paul wrote about to the Corinthians?

2. What does Ben learn about his father under the tree? How is Bull's attempt to make his son "tough"

misguided? Remember the song by Johnny Cash with a similar outlook, "A Boy Named Sue"? What view do Bull and the song have of the world?

3. Who in your family takes on the role of mediator? What quarrels or disputes have been defused by this person?

4. If there has not been such a person, where are the rifts, the broken places in your family, neighborhood, or community of friends where you might be the reconciler?

5. How are Ben's words to his father—"I love you! And there's nothing you can do about it!"—like the love we see in Christ on the cross? How does this unconditional love affect your own love and your relationships?

HYMN: "O Love that Will Not Let Me Go" or "When I Survey the Wondrous Cross"

A Prayer

Dear God, whose Son reached out in loving forgiveness even to cruel enemies mocking him at his execution, we confess that we are surprised by such love. We are more accustomed to resentment as a response to wrongs committed by or against us, rather than mercy. Give us the insight, the wisdom, the patience, and the love of a Lillian, that we might receive your peace, for ourselves and for others. We pray this in the name of the great Mediator, Jesus Christ, our Lord. Amen.

10. An Urban Good Samaritan
Grand Canyon

Rescue me from cruel and violent enemies, LORD!
   They think up evil plans and always cause
      trouble.
Their words bite deep
   like the poisonous fangs of a snake.

Psalm 140:1–3 (CEV)

So [the man] asked Jesus, "Who are my neighbors?"

   Jesus replied, "As a man was going down from
Jerusalem to Jericho, robbers attacked him and
grabbed everything he had. They beat him up
and ran off, leaving him half dead.

   A priest happened to be going down the same
road. . . ."

   Then Jesus asked, "Which one of these three
people was a real neighbor to the man who was
beaten up by robbers?"

Luke 10:29b–36 (CEV)

Introduction

In Lawrence Kasden's *Grand Canyon*, Mack, played by
Kevin Kline, is in a hurry to get home after attending
a pro basketball game. Trying to avoid the after-game
traffic jam, he drives off the freeway in search of a
shortcut through a deserted section of Los Angeles.
He becomes lost amid the unfamiliar streets of what
appears to be a warehouse section of the city. Then his
expensive car breaks down. He tries to call a tow service on his car phone, but it too malfunctions. Very
uneasy, especially when a car full of black teenagers

cruises slowly by, its occupants eyeing him, Mack walks to a pay phone and calls the tow service. The operator tells him it will be a while. Pleading with her to make it quick, he returns to his car to wait nervously for help to come.

The Scene

The Psalmist's cry "Rescue me from cruel and violent enemies, Lord!" could well be Mack's, as his worse fear is realized. The car full of teenagers passes by again, quickly turns around, and pulls up behind him. Mack's whispered prayer is more secular: "Mayday! Mayday! Going down!" The belligerent youth surround his car and, after some verbal sparring, order him out. Refusing at first, he obeys when the leader sticks a gun in his face and threatens him with bodily harm. An elderly black woman calls out of a passing car, "Leave that man alone," but the gang members merely laugh. Her driver keeps on going.

Before the gang can do anything further, the tow truck pulls up. The driver obviously can see what is transpiring, but he stops anyway. The camera allows us to see only the driver's cowboy boots and blue jeans–clad leg, thus leading us to expect a macho man who will teach these punks a lesson. Then we are allowed to see that the driver is a black man (played by Danny Glover). He is holding a tire iron, again leading us to believe that we will see a street fight, the tool making a good weapon. But the man makes no move that could be interpreted as belligerent or aggressive. Almost ignoring the challenge of the toughs, he goes about his work of hooking Mack's car to his truck. "Just trying to do my job," he replies to the upset and perplexed youth. He tells the relieved-looking Mack to get in his car. The gang leader is irritated even more when his buddies accuse the tow truck driver of "dissing him."

With his gun in prominent view, the gang leader talks with Simon (as we later learn is the tow truck driver's name). Simon explains that things are not supposed to be this way, that he should be able to go about his work, and the man shouldn't be threatened so. Then he asks that the leader grant him a favor, that he allow him to drive away with Mack without any trouble. Taken aback, the leader agrees, but demands that Simon first answer whether it is because of the gun that he respects him. Simon replies that "without the gun we wouldn't be having this conversation." "That's what I thought. That's why I have this gun!" the tough replies and then leaves with his friends. As Simon drives away with him, Mack breathes a sigh of relief and thanks his rescuer. Neither one knows it at the time, but this is the beginning of a remarkable friendship.

Reflection on the Scene

Less insightful writers than Meg and Lawrence Kasden would have turned this encounter into a Rambo or Jackie Chan fight, with the two good guys, both martial arts experts of course, easily beating up the bad guys. Simon's cowboy boots and jeans, which is what we first see of him, leads us to expect that, especially when we see the tire iron in his hand as he emerges from the truck. Instead, we are treated to an urban Good Samaritan episode, one in which the Samaritan comes upon a man *about* to be robbed, and in a gentle but courageous manner, patterned more after Gandhi or Christ than Rambo, talks the robbers out of committing their crime!

The Kasdens are among the rare breed of filmmakers who do not subscribe to the Rambo–Dirty Harry way of combating foes. They dare to suggest that there might be a better way of standing up to an aggressor than violence. Their Simon took a risk when he chose a conciliatory approach to the gang, much as Gandhi or Martin Luther King Jr. might have done. But his way is no riskier than the way of violent resistance, especially when in the real world it would be unlikely that either he or Mack would have known martial arts techniques. Simon's way could be followed by any of us, although it does require steady nerves and a belief that there is an alternative to violence in most situations.

For Further Reflection

1. Simon took a great risk in stopping to service the stranded Mack. He could have driven right by—after all, it was a white guy up against a gang of black men. Why do you think he stopped? Was it his dedication to his work as he understood it, greater than any fear or prejudice he might have had? Was it the values learned in church as a child?

2. Have you been in similar dire straits with no apparent way out? What were your feelings and thoughts at the time? Did you turn to prayer? What happened? How are imagination and courage important in finding a solution to a dilemma like Simon and Mack's?

3. What were your feelings toward your tormentors or opponents? Have you progressed in your spiritual life to the point of absorbing Christ's injunction to love your enemy? How does the scene show the wisdom of the ancient proverb that "a soft answer turns away wrath"?

4. The filmmakers refused to demonize Mack's tormentors and justify in the viewer's mind any mayhem committed against them by a Rambo-like hero. What is the significance of the gang leader's last statement? What does it reveal about his life and desires? How is all this helpful in the viewer's real life? In yours?

5. Have you been willing to take a risk as Simon did? How much in life are you willing to risk for the sake of your faith and neighbor?

6. In the wake of the terrible shootings at the high school in Littleton, Colorado, and other public places where youth congregate, a national debate on violence and youth has arisen. What do you think violent films contribute to our culture of violence? If you watch all of *Grand Canyon,* how do you think that Davis (played by Steve Martin), the maker of violent films, justifies his work? What are you and your church doing to overcome the many forces that promote violence in our society? Find out what organizations, schools, and churches are doing in your community to educate people in peacemaking. (Check with peacemaking programs in your community or at your church's denominational headquarters for resources they have produced. See the note in the Appendix for more information.)

HYMN: "God of Grace and God of Glory" or "Where Cross the Crowded Ways of Life"

A Prayer

Gracious and loving God, we thank you for your presence with us in moments of fear and danger. We are grateful that in film, as well as in Scriptures, you seek to lead us into a greater understanding of ourselves, our world, and even our faith. May we dare to trust you as we enter into those situations calling for risk and an understanding of others different from ourselves, and even of those who would exploit or harm us. Grant us courage, as well as wisdom and love, that we might truly be led in your ways of peace and justice. May the Holy Spirit inspire our imaginations that we might seek creative solutions to our conflicts. May we seek to become more than conquerors through Jesus Christ, who taught us to love enemies and to turn the other cheek when attacked. In his name, the Prince of Peace, we pray. Amen.

11. Costly Grace
Entertaining Angels: The Dorothy Day Story

Be merciful to me, O God, be merciful to me,
    for in you my soul takes refuge;
in the shadow of your wings I will take refuge,
    until the destroying storms pass by.
I cry to God Most High,
    to God who fulfills his purpose for me.
He will send from heaven and save me,
    he will put to shame those who trample on me.

God will send forth his steadfast love and
    faithfulness.

Psalm 57:1–3

"Whoever comes to me and does not hate father and mother, wife and children, brothers and sisters, yes, and even life itself, cannot be my disciple. Whoever does not carry the cross and follow me cannot be my disciple. For which of you, intending to build a tower, does not first sit

down and estimate the cost, to see whether he
has enough to complete it?"

Luke 14:26–27

Introduction

No one would have guessed that Dorothy Day would
become a great Roman Catholic social reformer when
she first came to New York City. She marches in a suf-
fragette parade and attacks supporters of Woodrow
Wilson. In Greenwich Village, the militant young
woman joins the circle of radical intellectuals that
included Eugene O'Neill, John Dos Passos, and John
Reed—all of whom disdain the church. She writes for a
Communist newspaper and enters into a love affair that
ends at a sleazy abortion clinic. In her articles she rails
against injustice but longs for a more fulfilling life. She
meets a man named Forster and lives with him on
Staten Island in a seashore cottage she was able to buy.
He tells her there will be no expectations or commitments, that theirs will be a relationship free of entangle-
ments. Despite their love, Dorothy still feels unfulfilled.

Then she meets a nun, Sister Aloysius, who runs a
soup kitchen where the poor gather and help to prepare their own meals. Dorothy is intrigued but still
hostile toward the organized church. She talks with the
nun and discovers a different type of faith than she had
envisioned, one that is warm and vibrant, looking to a
God who is "right in the middle" of the poor. Forster
is disapproving of her growing involvement with the
church. When their intellectual friends gather for a
picnic, he needles her and encourages the others in
their disparaging remarks about the church. This
upsets Dorothy, and she walks off. Forster tells her he
has to go into the city.

The Scene

Forster returns to the cottage to find Dorothy entertaining some of her new friends from the church kitchen. Revealing to Forster that she is pregnant, she says that she didn't think God would give her a second chance to have a child. Forster is upset that she brings God into this. Dorothy goes and sits quietly in the little church sanctuary. She is alone. After trying to pray silently, she says to herself that this is silly. She approaches the altar and, looking at the large crucifix on the wall, says accusingly, "You really sneak up on a person, don't you?"

In the next scene she is walking with Forster on the beach. He angrily asks why she is always "dragging God into everything." Dorothy has a baby in her arms, and we realize that months have passed and she is now a mother. "It's that nun!" Forster continues. "You're just confusing God with biology. It's motherhood that you feel!" He refuses to have anything to do with her "religious mumbo jumbo." Dorothy replies that all her life she has been drifting, that she doesn't want this for her child. She wants her to have something to hold onto, "to give meaning to her life." She pleads for him to be present at the baptism, but Forster refuses. He jumps into a boat and rows out against the incoming breakers. "I want you there," she calls out. Somewhat later Forster returns, saying that he wants to come back. Dorothy insists that they be married, "I need a commitment. *We* need a commitment!" Angrily declaring, "I won't be caged!" Forster stalks off.

In the little church, the priest prepares mother and child for baptism. Sister Aloysius is there, and so is the old hermit whom Dorothy had met on the beach and at church. But no Forster. Early the next morning she walks on the beach as the sun rises. She is silhouetted against a sky glowing with violet and red colors—alone.

Reflection on the Scene

Dorothy Day discovered the truth of what St. Augustine wrote at the beginning of his *Confessions:* "Thou has made us for thyself, and our hearts are restless until they find their rest in Thee." Neither her lovers nor her involvement in the intellectual gatherings nor her struggle for social justice through writing and demonstrations could fill the deep void in her life. And Forster's mocking of her struggle to find meaning in the church only intensified her longing. She had the misfortune to fall in love with a man who thought that he already had the answers, and who regarded God and the church as inimical to the quest for social justice. But through Sister Aloysius, who in one scene challenges Dorothy to read some books about the Christian faith and to make up her own mind, as well as the poor who come to the church to satisfy both their physical and their spiritual hunger, Dorothy finds God. She surrenders almost against her will, accusing Christ of sneaking up on her—through the nun and through the birth of her daughter.

But God has a rival in Dorothy's life, and his name is Forster. He is just as jealous as God. She has to choose between the two. And so she learns the awful truth of the hyperbolic words Jesus spoke to his disciples—that in comparison to the love and commitment they must have for him, their familial loves and commitments would seem like hatred. Turning to Christ, Dorothy had to turn her back on the man she loved. She had to "hate" Forster.

Many new followers of Christ have discovered this cost of discipleship. Christ changes their values and goals, but their friends or families still cling to the old. Angry words and accusations are hurled like weapons. Some of us who grew up in prejudiced families have found ourselves strangers at family gatherings, unable to accept racist remarks or to make those present understand our newfound beliefs. However, the new freedom discovered in Christ makes giving up the old more than worthwhile, even though there is pain involved. Dorothy's baptism into Christ is something she neither can nor wants to reverse, even if it means not getting Forster back. For God had indeed been merciful to her, surrounding her with "steadfast love and faithfulness."

For Further Reflection

1. When were you first aware that Christ was calling you? Were you always in the church, or like Dorothy did you come into faith from the outside? Who were the people who contributed to your faith development? A religious leader like Sister Aloysius or a lay leader? What books or Scripture passages aided you in your quest?

2. Why are so many people like Forster and his friends so hostile to God and the church? How is the church, which is supposed to be the means of bringing people to God, sometimes that which keeps them away from God? What is there about Sister Aloysius that attracted Dorothy and made her take another look at God and the church?

3. What does Dorothy mean when she says that God "sneaks up" on a person? How can God do this?

Through films, novels, dramas, poetry, music, and people? Note that the great lay theologian C. S. Lewis, once an atheist himself, wrote something similar in his autobiography *Surprised by Joy* that God is "unscrupulous" speaking to unbelievers through "open Bibles" and books. A person has to be very careful, he writes, if "he wants to stay an atheist!"

4. How is giving up Forster Dorothy's "cross"? Where in your spiritual journey have you encountered such a cross?

5. What meaning does your Christian faith bring into your life? How does Christ make your work and relationships with other people different from what they would be if he were not a part of your life?

HYMN: "Take Up Thy Cross" or "Called as Partners in Christ's Service"

A Prayer

Loving God, freely you give to us, and freely you offer your love. And yet when we turn to receive your gifts and when we accept your love, we find that we are changed. We no longer enjoy some of our old pleasures; the prejudices that made us feel superior and gave us unmerited advantages no longer enthrall us. When we become, in the words of your transformed servant Paul, a "new creation," others often seem confused and upset over our new condition. Help us to bear the pain of the new birth and to accept the cross of separation from families and friends who still think that a little faith might be all right, but a faith that turns our values upside down and inside out is too much. Save us from any self-righteousness or unctuous sanctimony, that we might, like Dorothy Day, lose ourselves in service to you and our neighbors in need. Through the Christ who took up his own cross and died for all, we pray. Amen.

12. Sweet-Sounding Grace
The Shawshank Redemption

How could we sing the LORD's song
    in a foreign land?

Psalm 137:4

Now hope that is seen is not hope. For who hopes for what is seen? But if we hope for what we do not see, we wait for it with patience.

Romans 8:24–25

Introduction

Andy Dufresne is a banker wrongly convicted of shooting his cheating wife and her lover. While serving a life sentence in Shawshank Prison, he befriends Red, a black man with connections on the outside. It is Red who narrates the events of the movie. When he first sees Andy, Red bets that Andy will be one of the first to break under the terrible prison conditions. But the former banker is made of sterner stuff than any of the older inmates could have guessed. Andy is sodomized by a gang but struggles to maintain his dignity and, above all, his hope. He writes a series of letters to the state authorities requesting funds for books for their inadequate prison library. By badgering them weekly for six years, he finally gets them to respond with money and boxes of used books. Among the treasures is an old phonograph and a stack of classical records. Andy is ecstatic to discover Mozart's *The Marriage of Figaro* among them.

The Scene

One day while cleaning the prison office, Andy is able to lock a guard in the bathroom and put on a record from the Mozart album. He turns on the prison public address system, and the lilting sound of a duet soars through the prison. Everywhere the men stop and listen to the haunting music. Even those unfamiliar with opera are mesmerized. As Red comments, "I have no idea to this day what them two Italian ladies were singing about. Truth is, I don't *want* to know. Some things are best left unsaid. I like to think they were singin' about something so beautiful it can't be expressed in words, and makes your heart ache because of it. . . . It was like some beautiful bird flapped into our drab little cage and made these walls dissolve away . . . and for the briefest of moments—every last man at Shawshank felt free."

Andy, of course, is overpowered by the guards and sent to solitary confinement for two weeks. Later he tells his friends that it was the easiest two weeks he ever did, for he had Mr. Mozart for company. When Red thinks that he had the record player, Andy taps his heart and head and says that the music was inside him where they could not confiscate it. He asks Red if he had ever felt that way about music, but Red, who once had played the harmonica, replies that he had given it up, that music doesn't make sense in prison. "Here's where it makes the most sense," Andy replies. "We need it so we won't forget." "Forget?" Red asks. "That there are things in this world not carved out of gray stone," says Andy. "That there's a small place inside of us they can never lock away, and that place is called hope."

Reflection on the Scene

Andy possesses a hope like that found in the Bible. He is sustained by memories of the outside, especially of its music, representing the beauty of the world. Instead of lamenting the injustices done him, in and outside of prison, he focuses on what cannot be seen and waits for it with patience, as the apostle Paul put it concerning the hope of the returning Christ. Of course, as those know who have seen the entire film, Andy does more than wait, but that is another story. It is his hope and his taste of freedom in beautiful music that sustains his efforts to chisel his way to the outside world. Long before he actually breathes the outside air, Andy is free, for he has been freed inside himself. His is like the freedom that Paul knows—a freedom that all who are, in Paul's words, "in Christ" can know.

"How could we sing the Lord's song in a foreign land?" Andy shows the way by staying connected with a world of beauty and hope that transcends the gray walls of his prison. We are not told much of Andy's faith, because the story is told by Red, who was not privy to this. We do know that Andy had a Bible, given by the hypocritical warden. But whatever its source, Andy's hope did indeed enable him to listen to, if not actually sing, "the Lord's song in a foreign land."

Few of us will wind up in a prison, like Andy, but we probably will find ourselves in situations that seem to imprison us: a dead-end job we long to escape; a lingering illness that seems intent on afflicting our body and spirit forever; a move to a hostile and strange place where we despair of ever finding a new friend. It is at such times that we desperately need the hope that sustained the apostle Paul and Andy. It is the hope that those who daily turn to Scripture and who join themselves to a worshiping community discover is theirs for the receiving.

For Further Reflection

1. What setbacks or disasters have banished you into a prisonlike status, "a foreign land"? Illness or disability? Loss of job or disappointment in love or friendship?

2. How did you feel at the time? Angry? Lamenting the injustice of it all? Despairing? Did feeling this way help anything? What or who sustained you? How and where did you find hope?

3. Has music played a similar role in your life? Hymns, airs from a piece of classical music, even a popular song of hope or joy can run through our minds regardless of our external circumstances. If you could pick one piece of music to share with others in a desperate situation, what would it be?

4. Andy acted on the urge to share his hope with the other prisoners. This proved to be a costly act. How is this like taking up the cross? In what ways have you shared your hope with others? Are you or your church helping those in the "foreign land" of a hospital, nursing home, or jail to sing "the Lord's song"?

5. Other films have also shown music to be a powerful force in sustaining hope: *Paradise Road*; *Philadelphia*; *Shall We Dance?*; *Fiddler on the Roof*; *Trip to Bountiful*. These would be good films to follow up this one, especially if your spirit needs some lifting.

HYMN: "Joyful, Joyful, We Adore Thee"

A Prayer

O God, the source of all hope, freedom, and love, we thank you for the artists who have created music and films that lift us out of ourselves, transporting us for a moment to your kingdom where there are no walls or brutality, and where ugliness is transformed into indescribable beauty. Sustain us by the hope that resides in your Son, that however and wherever we might find ourselves in some "foreign land," we might always know that you are close at hand. Prod us and move us to share that hope with others as well. This we ask in the name of the One who continually inspires hope within us, your Son, Jesus Christ, our Lord. Amen.

13. From Heel to Hero
Star Wars

> Then the LORD said to Cain, "Where is your brother Abel?" He said, "I do not know; am I my brother's keeper?"
>
> Genesis 4:9

> Then Jacob made a vow, saying, "If God will be with me, and will keep me in this way that I go, and will give me bread to eat and clothing to wear, so that I come again to my father's house in peace, then the LORD shall be my God, and this stone, which I have set up for a pillar, shall be God's house; and of all that you give me I will surely give one tenth to you."
>
> Genesis 28:20–22

Introduction

In *Star Wars*, Han Solo is a mercenary smuggler hired by Ben and Luke to transport them on their mission to find and rescue Princess Leia. She is an important leader of the rebel forces battling for freedom against the evil Empire. Han Solo, however, cares little about that. Money and his own safety are all that he cares for when we first meet him. Even after sharing a number of adventures with his companions, he decides to go his own separate way when the others get ready for a suicidal attack on the Death Star, the Empire's powerful weapon that threatens the freedom of the rebels. The gigantic Death Star, as large as an asteroid, houses a space cannon so powerful that it can destroy an entire planet. That is just what Darth Vader, commander of the Empire's forces, intends to do as soon as the huge satellite is maneuvered into position—destroy the entire planet on which the rebels have established their base.

The Scene

Near the end of the film, Luke is gearing up with his squadron for battle and, disappointed in Han's decision to go his own way, bids goodbye to him, as does Leia. The squadron's mission is a suicide one for many of the pilots, because their target is so tiny that they must fly in close above the surface of the Death Star in order to hit it. The rebels have obtained the plans of the mighty satellite and discovered that the only weakness in its defenses is a vent for an airshaft that leads deep into the heart of the Death Star. If a space torpedo can be shot into it, the missile will penetrate far enough to blow up the whole affair. But to get to it a pilot must fly down into a large trench, aim at the vent opening, and pull up immediately or be caught in the blast.

Cut to the thrilling climax of the attack, when Luke, piloting his fighter craft, is trying to concentrate on his dangerous approach to his target. Other pilots ahead of him have attempted the approach but either missed or were shot down. As he makes his approach into the trench, Luke fires, but misses. As he tries again, he finds that Darth Vader is on his tail, lining him up in his sights, ready to blow him to bits. Suddenly we hear a yell and catch just a glimpse of Han and his ship dropping down on Vader, his cannons finding their mark and sending the evil villain spinning out of control into space. Han, like a skilled blocker in football, has cleared the way for Luke to reach his goal. Aided by what he calls "The Force," the fighter pilot is able to complete his mission, scoring a bull's-eye with his torpedo. He barely has time to clear away from the Death Star before it is blown to pieces, thus safeguarding the freedom fighters from destruction. Back at rebel headquarters, Han joins his friends at the honors ceremony to receive a hero's reward.

Reflection on the Scene

Two of the most self-centered men in the Bible are Cain and Jacob. Adam's son Cain is so upset by his brother that he kills him, and when asked by God where Abel is, the first murderer utters that age-old, evasive question of the self-obsessed: "Am I my brother's keeper?" Jacob, too, is totally self-absorbed, his very name in Hebrew meaning "He who supplants," or just plain "Grabber." Fleeing from home because he has tricked his father and cheated his brother out of the family birthright, Jacob has a dream, a vision of grace during his first night away from home. But typically, the next day his vow-prayer centers on himself. He bargains with God. If the Lord will take care of Jacob and see that he prospers, he will be loyal to God. Only through long years of service and humiliation does Jacob finally come out of his self-centered shell, a transformation so radical that he is given a new name—Israel—which symbolizes his lifelong struggle with God.

Han Solo is very much like these two biblical characters. His very name marks him, even as Jacob's described his nature. "Solo"—alone. "Me, myself, and I" might well be his motto. Han does have a sidekick, like most cowboys, but it is significant that his companion is an alien who, as we see when he plays chess with the droids, is as self-centered as Han; he always must win. Han enters into the adventure with a "What's in it for me?" attitude; but as we see, he emerges a very changed man. It would have been neat in the sequel if George Lucas had given Han a new name, as God did Jacob after his epiphany in which he wrestled with an angel.

Han's "hero's journey," to use mythologist Joseph Campbell's term, is basically an inner one, taking place off-camera. It is the journey each of us must make, from self-centered childhood, through struggling adolescence, and finally into other-centered adulthood. It is the journey made by Jacob. It is the journey that Christ came to help us all make. In the Scriptures, it is a long way from Jacob's self-absorbed vow-prayer in the wilderness, "If God . . ." to Jesus' struggle in Gethsemane and his prayer, "If it be possible, God, take this cup from me, but nevertheless, thy will be done." But, as Han and Jacob learn, it is a journey well worth the effort.

May the Force of God's Spirit be with you as you journey from self to others to God.

For Further Reflection

1. Think back on your prayer life. How many of your prayers have been of the "give me" type? How or when did they begin to change? For what or for whom do you pray the most now?

2. Have there been role models to help inspire you to come out of yourself? Think about St. Francis, Dorothy Day, Albert Schweitzer, Dietrich Bonhoeffer, Mother Teresa, Martin Luther King Jr., Gandhi (to name some of my own).

3. Does your giving of time and money reflect this change? Does the surrounding culture support or undermine an "other-centered" lifestyle? For example, how many television and magazine advertisements seek to influence you to do something for yourself, rather than for others?

4. How can such groups as the church support you in your efforts? How do the traditional "means of grace"—prayer, the sacraments, and Scripture—aid you in your journey?

5. What have you been asked to do lately that you turned down? What were your reasons? Did the reasons deal more with inconvenience to you? Should you reconsider or give more thought to the next request?

6. If you have a recording of "One Is the Loneliest Number" by the group Three Dog Night, play it at the beginning or end of the session.

HYMN: "Take My Life and Let It Be" or "Gracious Spirit, Dwell with Me"

A Prayer

"Lord, make me an instrument of thy peace." We thank you, God, for such prayers and for the example of the lives of the saints who show us the way out of ourselves and lead us to you. We thank you that even in an escapist film like *Star Wars* you can speak to us, showing us a solo man answering your call to risk his safety for others. Continue to work in our own lives, overcoming our self-centeredness, leading us into a life of companionship, of "sharing the loaf" with others, for we ask this in the name of the One who is the Bread of Life, Jesus Christ, the Man for Others. Amen.

14. Waters of Mercy
Schindler's List

As a deer longs for flowing streams,
    so my soul longs for you, O God.
My soul thirsts for God,
    for the living God.
When shall I come and behold
    the face of God?
My tears have been my food
    day and night,
while people say to me continually,
    "Where is your God?"

Psalm 42:1–3

"Strike the rock, and water will come out of it, so that the people may drink."

Exodus 17:6b

"Whoever gives even a cup of cold water to one of these little ones in the name of a disciple—truly I tell you, none of these will lose their reward."

Matthew 10:42

Introduction

In Steven Spielberg's great Holocaust film, the German industrialist Oskar Schindler is transformed by his experience with his Jewish slave workers from a big-spending libertine into a caring human being. At the beginning of World War II, Schindler sought to profit from the war by taking over a Polish factory and using Jews to manufacture metal utensils for the German army. But he becomes so moved by the plight of a little girl during a roundup of Jews by the brutal SS that his conscience is stirred, and he begins protecting as many Jews as possible from being shipped off to the extermination camps.

The film has many moments of grace in which the German industrialist reaches out to help someone. This wonderful scene of grace is found at the end of the first tape. It is a terribly hot summer day, especially down at the train yard where a trainload of Jews bound for an extermination camp has stopped. We see close-ups of parched prisoners, more crowded than the cattle for which the car was built, crying out for water.

The Scene

Camp Commandant Amon Goeth and the other Nazi officers sit idly amusing themselves watching the train when Oskar Schindler joins them. They offer him a drink, and he chooses water. He watches the train, too, but unlike them, Oskar is moved to pity at the sight and sound of the parched prisoners begging for water. He asks that a fire hose be brought out. "Indulge me," he says. A crew, led by Oskar, hoses the train down. When the soldiers would move quickly on, Oskar orders "More!" The water drenches the occupants of the cars and cascades down through the roof into their parched mouths.

The officers roar with laughter at the spectacle, one of them joking, "Where's the fire?" Amon, still laughing, declares, "This is really cruel, Oskar. You're giving them hope." When the hose proves too short to reach the last cars of the train, Oskar remembers that he has some lengths back at his factory. It is brought up, and every prisoner is served. The prisoners in the cars, no longer crying piteously, continue to lick up whatever of the life-giving liquid they can catch. Quietly, Oskar gives the officer in charge of the station a basket of food and wine. He then instructs the officer to hose down every train that stops, for which there will be another basket sent to him. As the scene fades to black, the German officers have fallen into silence.

Reflection on the Scene

In many baptismal liturgies, there are references to the theological meanings of water: God's Spirit hovering over the waters at creation; the passage of Israel through the Sea of Reeds; water for the thirsty Israelites in the wilderness; the waters of Jesus' baptism; and Jesus' declaration that he is the living water. From the cross it is recorded that one of the last words of Jesus was "I thirst." Clearly, water is a basic part of life, but its meaning is more than just physical. This is especially the case in this scene, wherein water becomes a means of grace, a sign to a trainload of society's rejects that someone in the midst of a brutal, heartless world cares. Even the Nazi officers come to a dim awareness of this, their cynical laughter giving way to silence.

From Amon Goeth's point of view, giving water to the Jews is cruel, for he is very aware of the fate awaiting the unfortunate occupants of the train. Oskar Schindler knows this, too, and if he could have prevented their deaths, he would have. (Later he does go to great risk in saving several hundred of the women of his factory who have been sent to Auschwitz by mistake.) But he does what he can. He offers the prisoners the "waters of mercy." This might have been the only act of kindness they had experienced for a long time, and possibly the last. They had been torn from their homes, beaten and harangued, herded into cattle cars, packed so tightly that they could not sit. Many of them must have been driven to despair of all human kindness and hope. They will never know their benefactor, but at least their suffering was relieved for a moment.

There are times when one can do little to relieve the suffering of others. Life sometimes seems cruel and heartless, whether it be because of a bed of pain in some busy but lonely hospital or at an office ruled by an unfeeling boss imposing inhuman work rules. It is in such moments that even the smallest of kind acts takes on great meaning. These are connecting moments, moments of grace, when we are joined with another caring human being, reminded that we are not totally alone in our misery. And, through our faith we see that we are still connected with God. At such moments when, like the Psalmist's deer in the wilderness thirsting for water, we thirst, we long for such human connection. One simple act, even if it's just a smile or a nod of encouragement, can make a great difference. Maybe not in the final outcome—no more than Oskar Schindler could save the condemned Jews on that train—but at least for a brief span of time we are brought out of the terrible isolation of our inner wilderness suffering and joined with a caring human, and thus with a caring God.

For Further Reflection

1. Think back to one of your "thirsting" or desert experiences. Did you receive "waters of grace"? What form did this take? A smile, the touch of a hand, a small gift or service rendered?

2. How are even common courtesies—holding a door for someone or giving up a seat on a crowded bus—moments of grace?

3. Does the old story of Moses striking the rock and finding water make you think of ways in which God's grace has sustained you in the past?

4. What difficult situation that you cannot change can at least be alleviated by something you can do? Is there risk involved—maybe not as much as there was for Oskar Schindler, daring to be kind to Jews in front of a group of Nazis—but still the risk of ridicule or being misunderstood? Make a list of such situations and a list of what you could do. Pray, using the list as the content of your prayer.

5. The next time you witness a baptism, listen for the different references to water in either the introduction or the baptismal prayer.

HYMN: "As Pants a Hart for Cooling Streams" or "Where Cross the Crowded Ways of Life"

A Prayer

O God, through your waters of mercy you created our world, sustained your wandering children, and baptized us into your covenant people. I thank you for the Oskar Schindlers and the many unnamed and unknown people who have served as your conduits of the waters of mercy. Open my eyes, increase my faith and courage, as in love I seek to offer myself to you by joining in their efforts. When I can, help me to change harsh and difficult conditions that hurt people. And even when I cannot, help me still to bring some relief to those who thirst for kindness and love. In the name of him who is the Living Water, Jesus Christ, our Lord. Amen.

15. Bridge of Mercy
Babe: Pig in the City

Note: Many adults have watched neither Babe *nor its sequel,* Babe: Pig in the City, *on the mistaken assumption that these are "children's movies." Admittedly, they are accessible to children (though* Pig in the City *is a bit too dark for young children to watch alone), but these visual parable films are so full of spiritual insights that adults should not pass them by. They are too good to leave to the kids. Each offers a wonderful opportunity for adults to connect the wisdom of the film with that of Scripture and of life.*

> If your enemy is hungry, feed him; if he is thirsty, give him a drink. You will make him burn with shame, and the LORD will reward you.
>
> Proverbs 25:21–22 (TEV)

Wolves and sheep will live together in peace,
and leopards will lie down with young goats.

Calves and lion cubs will feed together,
  and little children will take care of them.
Cows and bears will eat together,
  and their calves and cubs will lie down in peace.
Lions will eat straw as cattle do.
Even a baby will not be harmed
  if it plays near a poisonous snake.
On Zion, God's holy hill,
  there will be nothing harmful or evil.
The land will be as full of the knowledge of the
  LORD
    as the seas are full of water.

Isaiah 11:6–9 (TEV)

"You have heard that it was said, 'An eye for an eye, and a tooth for a tooth.' But now I tell you: do not take revenge on someone who wrongs you. If anyone slaps you on the right cheek, let him slap your left cheek too."

Matthew 5:38–39 (TEV)

Never take revenge, my friends, but instead let God's anger do it. For the scripture says, "I will take revenge, I will pay back, says the Lord." Instead, as the scripture says, "If your enemy is hungry, feed him; if he is thirsty, give him a drink; for by doing this you will make him burn with shame." Do not let evil defeat you; instead, conquer evil with good.

Romans 12:19–21 (TEV)

Introduction

In this sequel to *Babe*, the little pig with "an unprejudiced heart" is traveling with his mistress by air to a city on another continent. Farmer Hoggett is facing financial difficulties that might result in foreclosure on the farm, so he accepts one of the many lucrative invitations for Babe to appear at a large fair. The sheep-herding little pig is now world famous, with many people clamoring to see the skills unheard of in a pig. Farmer Hoggett himself is laid up with an injury, so Mrs. Hoggett accompanies Babe. However, there is a mishap at a connecting airport, which causes the two to miss their flight. Because there are no more flights until some days later, Mrs. Hoggett takes Babe into the large city to look for lodgings. No one will accept pets, especially a pig. Their search appears hopeless, especially when the last lady of a small hotel located beside a canal refuses them in a voice that could be heard all over the neighborhood. It turns out that this was her intention, for she invites them from a side door to come in. She tells them that they can have a room, but that they must be careful lest her nosy neighbors across the street see them and report to the authorities that she is accepting nonhuman lodgers.

The two new arrivals are surprised to discover that the hotel is full of animals—dogs, cats, chimpanzees, monkeys, orangutans, birds, and a goldfish. The kind-hearted proprietor loves animals so much that she is willing to violate the city ordinance that prohibits hotels from taking in animals. She informs them that hers is the only place in the city to do so. Babe tries to make friends with the other animals, but they either ignore him or act coldly toward him.

Mrs. Hoggett goes into the city where she soon runs afoul of the law. She is thrown into jail and thus is unable to get back to Babe. The hotel lady also leaves for an errand that prevents her from returning. The only other human in the place is an ill-humored clown, and he dies. The animals are all alone, forced to fend for themselves. Some of them have some cookies and junk food, but nothing substantial, and even this they hoard, refusing to share. Hunger soon grips them all.

The Scene

Despite the danger of detection, the chimps decide to go outside to see if they can find anything to eat. Babe wants to go too, but they discourage him from accompanying them, telling him that a pig is useless. Babe denies this, telling them that he can herd sheep. One of the chimps says that he knows where there are some sheep. Babe follows his direction and enters a junk yard. He fails to notice the warning sign about a mean dog. Babe calls out the code signal for sheep, but there is no response except for a low rumble, like the beginning of a growl. It is too dark to see anything. Babe advances slowly toward the sound. Suddenly there is a vicious snarl and bark. Two snapping dogs lunge at Babe but are held in check by the chain attached to a stake. The dogs lunge again and again until they pull the stake out of the ground. By now Babe is running, the dogs in hot pursuit. The chimpanzees scatter, but the dogs stay on Babe's trail.

Down the street, past the hotel, and around the block the dogs pursue Babe. The little pig barely keeps ahead of them. At times the two dogs become entangled with each other and the long chain and stake. The chain and stake make a loud metallic, clanging noise, sometimes striking sparks on the stone pavement. At one point the chain snaps, and each dog is on his own. Several times they pass the hotel where the other animals, along with the chimps, stare out the windows at the spectacle. Not one makes a move to help the pig escape the horrible fate intended for him by the attack dogs, even though Babe is visibly tiring. One of the dogs has also become weary and drops out of the race. The other one, by far the meaner of the pair, keeps up the pursuit. Babe scrambles across the bridge over the canal and then, falling or jumping over the rail, plunges into the water. The lead attack dog follows him, apparently thinking he will catch his quarry in the water. However, the chain and the post become entangled in the railing of the bridge. Instead of diving into the water, the killer dog is now stuck, hanging head-down, his haunches and head beneath the surface of the canal. He struggles to release himself, but is helpless, the post holding fast to the railing. It appears that the end for the would-be killer is near.

The other animals merely watch, seemingly devoid of any concern, just as they had watched Babe flee without any offer of help. By now Babe has swum to the edge of the canal. He looks back and sees the predicament of the attack dog. Its struggles are becoming feebler by the minute. Without any hesitation the little pig swims back to where the dog is. With his snout he pushes a boat alongside the dog and then manages to maneuver the boat so that the dog's body is inside it. Babe and one of the monkeys revive the dog, who sputters back into consciousness. For a moment everyone is silent, seemingly taken aback by Babe's saving the very creature that had just tried to kill him.

Several stray dogs and cats have by now joined the animals from the hotel. Seeing the pig's magnanimous rescue of his enemy, they implore him for help. They tell Babe that they are the outcast and the friendless. One even begs, "Babe, save us!" Babe responds that he will try. He turns to the hotel animals, especially those holding onto their junk food and asks them to share with the street animals. None open their bags. The older chimp demands to know who gave Babe the authority to make such a request. Suddenly a loud voice draws the attention of all: "What the pig says, goes!" It is the attack dog, on his feet once more. He looks meaningfully and menacingly at the chimp and others. They all agree and slowly begin to share their meager stores of food.

Reflection on the Scene

Babe's act of grace at the bridge has won him a friend and supporter for life. Babe has destroyed his enemy by turning him into a friend. The junkyard dog has been changed by Babe's unexpected rescue. Long ago, the writer of Proverbs 25:21–22 understood this when he counseled treating an enemy with goodwill rather than revenge in the hope that the unexpected mercy would burn into the conscience of the enemy and extinguish all hostility. Without benefit of Scripture or teaching, Babe seems intuitively to know this. Little wonder that one of the desperate street animals regards him as a savior figure. This would not have happened had Babe walked away, leaving his attacker to his watery death. Nor would Babe have acquired a friend giving him such fierce support.

In his classic book *The Power of Non-violence*, Gandhian Richard Gregg describes Jesus' admonition to "turn the other cheek" as "moral jujitsu." Just as this Asian martial arts discipline is based on the surprising use of the opponents' strength and energy against themselves, thus throwing them off balance, so does refusing to return their hostility "throw them" psychologically and spiritually. According to Mr. Gregg, there is a basic agreement or compact between two sides that employ violence—namely, that violence is the only way to settle differences. (And in some cases, violence is even an enjoyable way. Remember Dirty Harry's words to the villain tempted to reach for a gun? With his huge Magnum pointed at the man, Harry urges, "Go ahead. Make my day!") With some important exceptions, this is the way differences and grudges are settled, with the physically stronger party defeating the weaker. But Jesus, in his Sermon on the Mount, teaches another way, the one followed by a little pig in our fantasy story. The story may be fiction, but its teaching is true. To return to Mr. Gregg, Babe has broken with the agreement that violence is the suitable way to deal with enemies. This leaves the enemy confused and off balance, because Babe has not acted like the stereotype in his mind. During the brief exchange between Babe, the street animals, and the hotel residents, the junkyard dog has regained consciousness and apparently gone through a metamorphosis. He enters the water regarding Babe as his enemy. He emerges from the water—as if baptized—realizing that his intended victim is a friend.

For Further Reflection

1. Were you surprised at Babe's act? Did he seem to have to think about what to do? If you have seen the first Babe movie, how is this consistent with the way he relates to others?

2. What are the other animals doing during the chase and subsequent struggle of the attack dog? Is such inaction typical? Why don't people want "to get involved"? Is there any sense of community before Babe comes along? Compare this at the present to what happens by the end of the film.

3. In the Scripture passages, note the difference in motivation for treating the enemy with kindness. The

author of the Proverbs passage is taking a pragmatic approach: treating the enemy thusly leads to practical results. Some commentators have even interpreted "the burning coals of fire" ("burn with shame," TEV) as being more vindictive than reconciliatory, more like the modern vernacular "bug the hell out of them." Jesus bases his admonition to "turn the other cheek" on his ethic of agape love, having instructed his followers a little earlier to love and pray for their enemy.

4. Which of the above do you think is more sustainable over the long haul if opponents refuse to let go of their hostility? Is there enough love within us to follow Jesus' ethic? Or do we need a source that transcends ourselves? The prayer attributed to St. Francis suggests the latter: "Lord, make me an instrument of thy peace. Where there is hatred, let me sow love; where there is injury, pardon."

5. Is there someone in your life whom you regard as an enemy, or who looks upon you as such? Think back over the relationship—or lack of one. What acts added to the hostility? What have either of you done to effect a reconciliation? Did this merely result in more hostility, with the attempt to reconcile rebuffed? Restoring a broken relationship or building a new one in the face of hostility requires a strong will and careful planning, much as a general might plan a difficult assault on a strongly held fortress. The following might prove helpful:

- Pray about the situation. Pray for yourself and the person who regards you as "the enemy."
- Think of as many good points of the opponent as you can and concentrate on them during any confrontation.

- Try to put yourself in the skin of your opponent so that you can see the situation from her or his viewpoint.

- Pick part of one of the sayings of Jesus, such as "Love your enemy," and repeat it like a mantra. The apostle Paul's "I can do all things through him who strengthens me" is also helpful.

- Seek the support, including prayers, of your community, whether friends in or out of the church.

- Seek out opportunities to talk over your differences: ask for and/or give forgiveness.

- Do some act of kindness for the would-be friend (and regard the opponent in this way).

- Keep in your mind a vision of a restored or new friendship, using Second Isaiah's poetic image of the restored harmony in nature as a model.

- Keep on praying, for the reconciliation campaign might take a long time and a lot of energy.

It should also be noted that the campaign might not be successful as you hope. Some hearts become so shriveled over time or so full of hostility that it is beyond our power to change them. The most famous practitioner of Jesus' love ethic, Mohandas Gandhi, although pointing to the often practical results of what he called *satyagraha* ("soul" or "truth force"), always maintained that he would rather be hurt himself than hurt another, including an opponent. Paul wrote to the Romans that "in so far as it is possible" with them they should "live in peace" with their neighbors. Even if the campaign does not make an enemy a friend, it should not be deemed a failure, for it will prevent you from becoming bitter or nursing old wounds or grudges.

HYMN: "They'll Know We Are Christians by Our Love"

A Prayer

Gracious God, you created us in your image and placed us in a beautiful garden to care for it and one another in accordance with your loving will. But we rebelled against your gentle way and turned your garden into a jungle where the strong devour the weak. Denying that we are our brother's keeper, we have competed against one another in hostility that too often has erupted into violence, in the illusion that yours is a world of scarcity rather than abundance. We thank you for the writers and prophets of Scripture who taught of a way out of the violence that has so escalated that it threatens us today with annihilation. We are especially grateful to you for sending us your Son, who not only taught but embodied your way of nonviolence, the result of which will be a world in which the strong and the weak, the one-time predators and their prey, will lie down together in harmony. Give us your Spirit that we will join with others in the acceptance and the proclamation of this Peaceable Kingdom. In the name of the Prince of Peace we pray. Amen.

16. The Wounded Healer
The Spitfire Grill

He was oppressed, and he was afflicted,
    yet he did not open his mouth;
like a lamb that is led to the slaughter,
    and like a sheep that before its shearers is silent,
    so he did not open his mouth.

By a perversion of justice he was taken away,
  Who could have imagined his future?
For he was cut off from the land of the living,
  stricken for the transgression of my people.

Isaiah 53:7–8

For the hurt of my poor people I am hurt,
  I mourn, and dismay has taken hold of me.

Is there no balm in Gilead?
  Is there no physician there?

Jeremiah 8:21–22a

Then he said to Thomas, "Put your finger here
and see my hands. Reach out your hand and put
it in my side. Do not doubt but believe."
Thomas answered him, "My Lord and my
God!"

John 20:27–28

We are treated as impostors, and yet are true; as
unknown, and yet are well known; as dying, and
see—we are alive; as punished, and yet not killed;
as sorrowful, yet always rejoicing; as poor, yet
making many rich; as having nothing, and yet
possessing everything.

2 Corinthians 6:8b–10

Introduction

Percy Talbot, fresh out of prison, wins the support of
Hannah, owner of the Spitfire Grill where Percy works
as a waitress, and Shelby Goddard, who is married to
Hannah's nephew Nahum. Nahum is overly protective
of his aunt and deeply suspicious of Percy's motives in

helping the older woman. He cannot understand why Percy would want to come to such a small town as Gilead unless she had learned about his aunt and had decided to take advantage of her. He begins calling out-of-town contacts to try to find out why she had been imprisoned. He also is resentful of the liberating effect Percy has on his once-docile wife, whom he had so long derided and taken for granted.

Although she becomes a channel of grace for the two women, Percy herself is troubled by her dark past. She tells a cryptic story about an Indian mother and her child drowned in a canoe. Only later, when she opens up to Shelby and reveals that she had been abused, raped, and impregnated by her stepfather, do we begin to understand the strange and sad story. Percy had promised the child in her womb that she would protect it, but when it died because of the beatings she had received from her stepfather, she fell into despair, blaming herself for her failure to keep her promise to protect it. Finally, in self-defense, she killed her tormentor during one of his assaults.

The Scene

Hannah, while climbing on a chair to reach a closet shelf, loses her balance and falls. Hearing her cry, Percy rushes up to her room. Hannah tells her to leave her alone, but Percy, seeing that the older woman's ankle is injured, takes charge, calling the emergency squad. Hannah is laid up, unable to work, and it is during this recuperative period that Percy proves herself so useful, both to Hannah and to Shelby, who comes to help out in the Grill. One evening, while rubbing ointment on Hannah's leg, Percy asks, "Are there some wounds so deep that the healing hurts worse than the wound?" Hannah has no answer to this obviously heartfelt query. Later Percy sings the song that for her is more like the question Jeremiah originally intended it to be, "There Is a Balm in Gilead."

Reflection on the Scene

Percy is able to help Hannah at the grill and restore Shelby's crushed spirit, while at the same time suffering inner pangs of guilt and remorse. She tells Shelby that God could never forgive her for her failure to protect her baby. It might seem paradoxical that someone so deeply wounded herself can be such a channel of healing for Shelby and—in the subplot dealing with Hannah and her mentally ill son—for Hannah also. Percy's question is a theological one, although she does not fully comprehend it. In the cross, which Jesus reluctantly accepted at Gethsemane, the wound—sin so deep that it threatened the future of the human race—is healed. But the healing, involving the death of the innocent Son of God, must have hurt God "worse than the wound." Hundreds of years earlier during the depth of Judah's apostasy, Jeremiah sees his countrymen's moral sickness as so deep that he cries out in anguish, "Is there no balm in Gilead?" It is not until a few years later that another prophet, living in Babylon with the exiled people, sees that there is a physician for the people, a strange Servant whom he describes as "oppressed and afflicted," a servant who would suffer on behalf of his people, and thus, through the wounds of his own back, bring healing. No wonder that the church saw this Servant as being fulfilled in the life, death, and resurrection of Jesus of Nazareth!

Percy's story is very much like that of the Suffering Servant and of the apostle Paul in our Scripture passages. Nahum treats her as an impostor in the mistaken belief that she is out to steal his aunt's money. Yet she "makes rich" others who see the goodness within her: Shelby is brought out of her submissive shell; Hannah is led to see how she can fulfill her dream to sell the Spitfire Grill; and even more important, Hannah and her son, mentally damaged by the Vietnam War, are reunited. Even Joe, a would-be suitor of Percy, is brought to a new awareness of his surroundings. But, like the resurrected Christ who still bears the deep marks of his suffering, Percy bears the mark of her crucified past, an open wound in her life needing the balm of Gilead. For her, healing will come only through death, a death not unlike that of the Suffering Servant, whose sacrifice brought healing to his people Israel and then to the whole world.

For Further Reflection

1. If you were Hannah, what might you have said in answer to Percy's question? As you have been with people at wakes and funerals, what similar questions have you heard—or perhaps asked yourself?

2. What easy answers do people give sometimes to questions about suffering and death? How can these be more harmful than helpful? What might be best—not to answer at all; to offer tentative ones; or simply to be there, perhaps offering a prayer and a hug?

3. How have you seen good coming out of suffering? "Good" for whom? The sufferer, or those around the afflicted person?

4. In what sense are we all called to be "wounded healers"? Who are some of the wounded healers in your church or group, or in your past?

5. Meditate on the words of Isaac Watt's great hymn, "When I Survey the Wondrous Cross."

See, from his head, his hands, his feet, Sorrow and
love flow mingled down.
Did e'er such love and sorrow meet, Or thorns
compose so rich a crown?

6. To go deeper into the theme, read Henri Nouwen's fine book, *The Wounded Healer.*

HYMN: "There Is a Balm in Gilead" or "When I Survey the Wondrous Cross"

A Prayer

O God, our compassionate Creator, you entered into our human existence and took upon yourself the suffering for the whole world. As we confront the mystery of human pain and misery, help us always to remember the passion of our Lord Jesus, your Son, "cut off from the land of the living," yet who emerged victorious in your resurrection power, still bearing the wounds of his love and our hate. We seek not easy answers that satisfy the questions of our minds, but instead the assurance of your presence to be with us and those with whom we stand in the midst of pain and confusion. This we ask in the name of your Son, the Wounded Healer, Jesus Christ, our Lord. Amen.

17. Ennobling Grace
Dead Man Walking

But now thus says the LORD
    he who created you, O Jacob,
    he who formed you, O Israel:
Do not fear, for I have redeemed you;
    I have called you by name, you are mine.
When you pass through the waters, I will be with
    you;
    and through the rivers, they shall not over-
        whelm you;
when you walk through fire you shall not be
    burned,
    and the flame shall not consume you.

Isaiah 43:1–2

Then Jesus said to the Jews who had believed in
him, "If you continue in my word, you are truly
my disciples; and you will know the truth, and
the truth will make you free."

John 8:31–32

But God proves his love for us in that while we
still were sinners Christ died for us. Much more
surely then, now that we have been justified by his
blood, will we be saved through him from the
wrath of God. . . . For all who are led by the Spirit
of God are children of God.

Romans 5:8–9; 8:14

Introduction

Sister Helen Prejean has agreed to be the spiritual
guide for convicted rapist-killer Matthew Poncelet.

Hers is not a popular decision. Her parents, colleagues, and clients at the city community center
where she works all question whether she should be
associating with such a hardened criminal. The parents of the young couple so savagely killed by
Poncelet and his friends especially are upset by her
ministering to the spiritual welfare of a man they
would like to see executed. Sister Prejean, however,
believes in the radical love of God, who extends a
grace "so amazing, so divine" that it includes even
Matthew Poncelet.

Poncelet, playing the role of the hardened tough
guy, refuses to accept responsibility for his crime. He
blames everyone—his parents, his companions, even
the victims themselves for being there in that iso-
lated place—everyone but himself. Also, Poncelet is
firm in denying that he is in any way "a victim." But
Sister Prejean, imitating poet Francis Thompson's
"The Hound of Heaven," will not let him escape.
Even when he tells her "Me and God are O.K,"
Sister Prejean refuses to accept this. She wants him
to face the truth about himself and what he did. It is
only by participating in his redemption and accepting the truth that he can find the freedom that Christ
promises, she tells him. The bad news that his
appeals have been turned down forces Poncelet to
face up to his fate.

The Scene

Near the end of the film, Poncelet finally admits that
he did not walk away from his friends during the
killing. "I was a victim," he says—but this is not a
dodge of responsibility. To her question "Do you take
responsibility for their deaths?" he responds that he

does. "You did a terrible thing, but you have a dignity now. Nobody can take that from you. You are a son of God." Matthew cries as he says, "Nobody ever called me that before."

Later, just before his own death by execution, he tells Sister Prejean, "I have to die to find love. Thank you for loving me!" She assures him that she will be there at his death—and that God will be too. On the way to the death chamber, she reads from Isaiah God's promise that "the waters" will not overwhelm him because of the loving presence of God.

Reflection on the Scene

Society reminds us always that there are those who are "in" and those who are "out," those who are acceptable and those who are unacceptable by reason of race, economic and social status, nationality, political or religious beliefs, and, above all, by their moral status. Certainly, rapists and killers are in the outermost circle, totally unacceptable. Yet Sister Prejean is bound not by society's dictates, but by the teaching and example of Jesus of Nazareth. She allows herself to be drawn into the life of Matthew Poncelet despite the protests of everyone around her. She learns that beneath his tough exterior there is a very vulnerable human being.

Her example and Jesus' example can help us in two ways: First, by reminding us that when we think or do shameful things God still loves us. He is not the Cosmic Policeman and Judge eagerly waiting to strike us down and consign us to the fires of hell when we step out of line. Instead, he is the loving Creator, who like the father in Jesus' parable, rushes out to welcome back the returning son. Second, their story encourages us to show that same kind of love to others, even those regarded as totally unworthy and undesirable. As we see by the spiritual struggle of Matthew Poncelet, neither is easy. But to know the truth that will make us free, we must face up to our own unworthiness and the fact that we are still accepted by a loving God. As theologian Paul Tillich has put it, we must "accept our acceptance"—and the acceptance by God of others as well.

For Further Reflection

1. How pervasive is the belief that we must be acceptable in order to be accepted by God and society? When was the last time you heard someone say (maybe yourself), "Boy, I must be doing something (right, or wrong), everything's going (right, wrong) lately"? Note how the pitch of ads for such personal grooming products as deodorants is based on the desire to be acceptable. How do even churches at times show that some people are more acceptable than others?

2. Is there something in your life of which you are ashamed, for which you have denied responsibility? A sin of commission or omission? Words uttered in anger or with no thought of their consequences? The past cannot be altered, but the present can be changed by facing up to past misdeeds or faults. What can you do to change the consequences? How does beginning with God help?

3. Read or sing again the words of John Newton's great hymn, "Amazing Grace." If he, a former captain of a slave ship, could be transformed by God's love, is there anything in your life that need enslave you?

4. Is there someone in your life with whom you have broken a relationship because of his or her past misdeeds or present practices? What can you do to bridge the chasm?

5. Sister Prejean agrees to serve as Matthew Poncelet's spiritual adviser. Why is this a good, and growing, practice? Is there someone wise and mature to whom you can turn to share your spiritual journey, your questions, temptations, and confessions?

HYMN: "Amazing Grace" or "Just as I Am Without One Plea"

A Prayer

Gracious God, how often we pass over these two words—*gracious* God! Not wrathful or condemning God, but gracious God. Your love that reaches out to us through Jesus upon the cross always seems "so amazing, so divine" when we encounter it. Help us to acknowledge our own failure to see the truth of our own unworthiness and the greater truth of your love. Realizing how much we are loved, help us by your Spirit to love all others whom we meet, no matter how unworthy we or the world think they are. We pray this in the name of the One who embodied your love, Jesus Christ, our Lord. Amen.

18. Easter Means a Second Chance
Field of Dreams

Now the LORD said to Abram, "Go from your country and your kindred and your father's house to the land that I will show you."

Genesis 12:1

When the LORD restored the fortunes of Zion,
    we were like those who dream.
Then our mouth was filled with laughter,
    and our tongue with shouts of joy.

Psalm 126:1–2a

But just as we have the same spirit of faith that is in accordance with scripture—"I believed, and so I spoke"—we also believe, and so we speak, because we know that the one who raised the Lord Jesus will raise us also with Jesus, and will bring us with you into his presence.

2 Corinthians 4:13–14

Introduction

At the beginning of this 1989 fantasy, Iowa farmer Ray Kinsella hears a voice telling him, "If you build it, he will come." Like Abram of old, Ray struggles and then obeys the voice. At first his journey is not as long as Abram's, just out to his cornfield. He believes that the mysterious Voice is calling him to build a baseball field. To the amazement of his neighbors, he gives over valuable cropland to the ball field, a "field of dreams." The "he" who "will come" turns out to be Shoeless Joe Jackson, accompanied by his teammates of the infamous Chicago "Black Sox," the team that had thrown the 1919 World Series because of a dispute with their unfair team owner. When the plot was uncovered, the players had been banned forever from professional baseball, so the team now welcomes a chance to play on a ball field again.

The Scene

Ray soon learns that it is not just for this team that he has been called. He is sent on a real journey to "ease his pain," discovering in a far city Terence Mann, a writer who had been the conscience of his generation during the Sixties but who had withdrawn from society in defeat and pain. Ray and the writer travel to Minnesota to encounter still another person with unfulfilled dreams, a doctor who had given up his chance to play professional baseball in order to return to his hometown and minister to the people there. The three return to the farm and join the team on the field.

Ray finds that dealing with his own sense of unfulfillment is also a part of his call. He is reunited with the father with whom he had never been at ease. Indeed, during the rebellious Sixties they had broken off contact, and his father had died. Ray realizes that his father too had had unfulfilled dreams of breaking out of the minor leagues and playing ball in the majors. In a beautiful night scene, Ray gets a second chance to be reconciled with his father, even as all the others had received second chances on the Field of Dreams.

Ray has been plagued by the disbelief and ridicule of his unbelieving brother-in-law, who has been urging his impractical relative to sell the farm. But then, when Ray's little daughter is injured, she is cured by the ball-playing doctor. In a moment of epiphany, the brother-in-law too finally "sees" the ball players and supports

Ray's decision not to sell. At the end of the film, we see a long procession of approaching car lights; they fulfill in still another way the promise of the mysterious Voice, "If you build it, he will come."

Reflection on the Scene

Although there is little or no religious language in the film and thus no mention of God or Christ, this film is a visual parable of Easter faith proclaimed by the apostle Paul to the Corinthians. The universe of the story is a spiritual one of grace, of possible second chances. The mysterious Voice is never identified, the filmmakers leaving it up to viewers to provide their own interpretation. The film was an enormous success, and each year thousands of people visit the "field of dreams" in Iowa, because the story tapped a deep desire in all of us who wish for a second chance in life: a second chance to put right a relationship with a dead parent, as in Ray's case; or to follow an untrod path, as in the doctor's case; or to recapture the courage and joy of past commitments, as in the cases of the writer and the disgraced baseball team. *Field of Dreams* assures us in its secular-spiritual way that the basic message of Easter is true. Death in all its forms— alienation from loved ones, disgrace, and failure—has been overcome.

He might not recognize it, but Ray shares with the apostle Paul "the same spirit of faith as he who wrote, 'I believed, and so I spoke.'" Ray's faith response was to build a ball field and then to set forth on a journey into the unknown. As with Abram, it was a journey with many unexpected consequences. It was a journey into, and sustained by, an Easter faith.

For Further Reflection

1. It has been reported that thousands of people stop by the Iowa farm where the film was shot. Why do you think they do this? With what inside of them did the film connect?

2. What memories of your own parents does the film bring to mind? What unfulfilled desires and dreams do you have? Do you have broken relationships that need mending?

3. The mysterious Voice is never named or identified. What do you make of it? If it is not God, then what is it? Think about your own spiritual journey. At what points in your life have you had a mysterious experience, some nudging of your will, quickening of spirit, or burst of insight that made a difference in your life? If you have a copy, read Dag Hammarskjöld's journal entry "Whitsunday, 1961" in *Markings* (New York: Random House, 1966, p. 205). Note that he at first does not identify the "Someone" to whom he was led to say "Yes." But then, toward the end of his meditation, he does identify the "Someone." Who is it?

4. At the beginning of his quest, Ray is supported by his wife, Annie. She tells him that she thinks it's weird, but that he must set out. How important is the support of others in our spiritual development? Ray also finds companions along the way. Where have you received support and companionship in your own spiritual quest? Who among the people at your church seem to be searching still?

5. How is Ray's quest similar to that of Abram and Sarai? To your own? How is Ray's story also an Easter story? Where do you see "resurrection" in his

life? What are the tombs in your life in need of a resurrection?

6. How does your faith in the resurrection of Christ get you through difficult times? Seeing that we do not live in a fantasy story like Ray's, what can you do about an unresolved relationship with someone who has died?

HYMN: "The God of Abraham Praise" or "O God in a Mysterious Way"

A Prayer

Dear God, you reach out to your children in many and wonderful ways, calling us forth on journeys of faith and discovery. We thank you for Abram and Sarai and their example, and for the apostle Paul, whose journey of hatred was interrupted by your risen Son, turning the persecutor around and sending him forth instead on journeys of love and grace. You are the searcher of all hearts, so you know our longings and desires, our disappointments and broken and unfulfilled dreams. Enter into our hearts so that we might experience a sense of acceptance and fulfillment, as promised to all who turn to you. Transform our fields of defeat or disappointment into fields of dreams dedicated to your service and thanksgiving. We pray this in the name of the Easter Christ. Amen.

19. A Father's Love
The War

Hear, my child, your father's instruction,
　　and do not reject your mother's teaching;
for they are a fair garland for your head,
　　and pendants for your neck.

Proverbs 1:8–9

As a father has compassion for his children,
　　so the LORD has compassion for those who
　　　　fear him.
For he knows how we were made;
　　he remembers that we are dust.

Psalm 103:13–14

God is love, and those who abide in love, abide
in God, and God abides in them.

1 John 4:16b

Introduction

In director Jon Avnet's *The War*, Kevin Costner plays Stephen, father of an adolescent son and daughter. At times Stu and Lidia have difficulty understanding their father, a Vietnam veteran who returned from the war deeply traumatized. He cannot hold a job for long, especially when it is learned that he has spent time in a mental ward. Fortunately, his wife, Lois, loves him deeply and stands by him loyally.

Stephen has a strong aversion to violence of any kind, and this also creates misunderstanding between him and Stu and Lidia. The children have to contend with the Lipnickis, the bane of their existence. The six roughneck kids are the sons and daughter of the mean owner of the local junkyard. Stu, Lidia, and their friends are constantly at war with the belligerent gang, especially when the former build a fort in a magnificent tree. When the Lipnickis discover it, they want it for themselves. The "war" of the title thus refers not only to the adult Vietnam War but also to the war over possession of the tree house.

The Scene

Following an incident with the Lipnicki children and their father at the county fair, Stephen and Stu have a long father-and-son talk. Stephen tells his son that it is wrong to fight, but Stu reminds his father that Stephen himself was in the war; Stephen was a hero serving his country to keep everyone safe. Stephen reveals then what has been haunting him from the war—how he had carried his wounded best friend through falling shells and gunfire to the medivac helicopter, only to be told that there was room for just one more in the overloaded chopper. The pilot urged Stephen to leave his friend, because it was evident that he was dying. There was little time to debate; the enemy troops were closing in fast. Stephen nevertheless argued, begged, even leveled his pistol at the pilot, but to no avail. Crying, he lay his buddy on the ground and climbed into the chopper. The memory of the receding body of his friend far below continues to haunt and torment him.

After a moment of crying, Stu hugs his father, and Stephen continues, "I can't tell you never to fight, Stu. But whether or not you want to know what I think—I think the one thing that keeps people truly safe and happy is love. I think that's where men get their courage, and that's where countries get their strength, and that's where God grants us our miracles. And in the absence of love, Stuart, there's nothing, nothing in this world worth fighting for."

Reflection on the Scene

The War is one of the rare films that challenges the old way of relating to enemies. It takes a lot more conflict and heartache before Stu comes to understand and accept his father's values. Growing up in a society that prizes physical strength and honors violence, Stu finds it difficult to change his ways. He is aided by his father's teaching and example. Later, in a mine cave-in, Stephen faces a dilemma similar to his Vietnam experience. This time he refuses to leave a friend pinned down by rubble, a decision that turns out to be a very costly one. Shortly after this Stu finds himself in a situation in which he must decide whether to risk his life when the youngest of the Lipnickis is caught in a powerful whirlpool high up in an old water tower.

Even while claiming allegiance to the Christ of the New Testament, many of us regard his teaching to love our enemies as impossibly idealistic. Stephen and Stu learn that war, whether in the adult or the smaller-scale children's version, leads only to destruction. Even if we win, we are nothing without love. The New Testament ethic actually is one of survival for a world wracked by violence. Love, far from being weak, is the only force capable of overcoming our prejudices and hatreds. When the love of God and neighbor motivates us, we relate to enemies in new and creative ways. Stu is blessed with a father who teaches and lives the way of love. All of us are blessed with a God who is the source of that love. The life and death of Christ demonstrate a love so great that no enemy, not even death, can overcome it. Persistent love destroys enemies by trans-forming them, at least in our minds and hearts, into brothers and sisters.

For Further Reflection

1. Was yours the kind of father with whom you could have such a talk? If your father passed to you any special thoughts or values, what were they? (Some-times, too, a father can impart negative values, such as racial prejudice, as in *American History X*. How have you dealt with this?)

2. Compare Stephen's words to his son with the words in 1 John 4 or 1 Corinthians 13. Are there Lipnickis in your life? How is dealing with them in love better than reacting to them with hostile means?

3. Stephen was caught in a wartime situation beyond his control, yet for which he bore tremendous guilt. Are there past events in your life that have left you feel-ing like Stephen? How has the image of a loving, for-giving God helped you deal with these? Do you each day seek God's guidance and forgiveness in prayer?

4. *The War* teaches the way of love and reconcilia-tion, yet many films are based on the sweetness of revenge. What films of the latter type can you think of? Why is revenge self-defeating in the long run? For example, what has it gained in Ireland, the Balkans, or Palestine?

5. Reread Stephen's words to his son. How would you handle a child's problem of dealing with a school bully? Can praying and love help in such a situation? What creative solution might be found? Do you have to seek one by yourself, or can other parents and adults at church or in the neighborhood also be of help? For an excellent film showing parents and a

minister counseling a boy how to deal with a belligerent kid, see Feature Films for Families' *The Butter
Cream Gang.*

HYMN: "Eternal Power, Whose Power Upholds" or
"O God of Love, O God of Peace"

A Prayer

Creator God, you are love, and you sent us your Son
to show us the way of love. Often we continue the old
ways of relating to enemies, returning insult for insult,
blow for blow, thus perpetuating old divisions and ani-
mosities. So fill us with your Spirit that we will dare to
accept your way of love and reconciliation. As we think
of someone or some group, some broken relationship,
help us see them with new eyes. Stir our own imagination that we might be as creative in the way of peace as
others are in the ways of resentment and vengeance. In
the name of the One who reconciles us through the
cross, Jesus Christ, our Lord. Amen.

20. Blessed Are the Merciful
The River

As a deer longs for flowing streams,
    so my soul longs for you, O God. . . .
As with a deadly wound in my body,
    my adversaries taunt me,
while they say to me continually,
      "Where is your God?"

Psalm 42:1, 10

A soft answer turns away wrath,
    but a harsh word stirs up anger.

Proverbs 15:1

"Blessed are the merciful, for they will receive mercy."

Matthew 5:7

Introduction

Tom and Mae Garvey are desperately trying to hold on to their Tennessee farm. They love farm life and want to pass it on to their two children. But they must battle both natural and human foes. When Tom learns that a steel mill in the city is offering jobs, he decides to go, even though it will mean being away from family and farm for a long time. However, his relief at finding a job that will pay enough money to keep the farm going is tempered by the discovery that the new workers are replacing those who went out on strike. The company is using the new workers to break the union and its efforts to better the lot of mill workers. Just as the striking workers were locked out of the plant, Tom and his coworkers are locked in by the company. From inside they can hear the angry cries of "Scab!" hurled at them by the strikers, who would love to attack them.

Tom becomes acquainted with several coworkers on his shift and during the leisure hours in which they are cooped up in their crowded dormitory. No one is allowed during the week to venture outside the fence protecting them and the plant from the angry union members. When one young worker, anxious to get to his wife who is about to give birth to their first child, climbs over the fence and sets off to join her, he is set upon by a group of strikers. Tom and several other strikebreakers hastily scramble over the fence and rescue him.

The Scene

One day a worker looks up and spots a young deer that has wandered into the plant. He and his friends drop their tools and chase after it. As the deer runs down the center of the plant, other workers join in the chase, some of them trying to capture the animal with flying tackles. Filled with the thrill of the hunt, all of the workers converge on the deer, their bodies forming an impenetrable wall surrounding it. From atop a mound of dirt, it looks around in confusion and fear.

The men stop and silently stare at the deer. They can see the fear in its large, brown eyes. The creature's body begins to tremble. The poor animal is so frightened that it loses control of its bladder and urinates. The men stare quietly for a few more moments. Then, without any word or signal, those closest to the open door of the building step back, on either side creating an aisle, down which the frightened animal runs. Soon it is bounding to freedom in the field beyond the plant.

Shortly thereafter the foreman comes around to announce that the strike is over. The workers are to pick up their pay immediately and leave the grounds. The men look for the trucks that had brought them safely through the picket line into the plant. They are not there, and they won't be, the foreman tells them. That was part of the deal the striking workers had insisted on being part of the settlement—no trucks for the scabs. Tom and his coworkers must walk out on their own. When the men protest, the foreman calls for the plant security guards, who force the men toward and then through the gate.

Tom and his coworkers stand looking at the picketers.

The union members, many of them holding clubs and sticks, stare back in hostile silence. There is a long stand-off, and then the picketers part to form a long aisle. We wonder if it will become a gauntlet for the besieged men. The released workers slowly walk toward the union members and enter the passageway. No one raises a club, but a few, especially some of the women, yell "Scab!," and one spits directly into Tom's face. He and his coworkers look down, none of them returning a word. They emerge from between the two lines of their tormentors unscathed, except for a lessening of their sense of dignity and self-respect.

Reflection on the Scene

Normally, most of the meat-hungry workers would not have hesitated to kill the deer to put meat on their family tables as well as for the sheer thrill of the kill. Out in a field or woods, armed with a rifle, they could have killed it with one or two shots from fifty or sixty yards. But in the close confines of the mill, with the trapped quarry just a few feet away, they could see its fear. They seemed to realize that the poor animal was in a situation identical to their own—trapped, cornered by enemies intent on doing them harm. Slowly their compassion arose, becoming stronger than their desire for fresh meat or the urge to hunt and kill.

Something similar must have occurred in the hearts and souls of the vengeance-seeking strikers. When they had their opportunity to get even with the scabs who prolonged the strike by taking their places and keeping the plant operating, they held back. There were no trucks or guards to protect the strikebreakers. The picketers far outnumbered them. But the picketers let the scabs go. Perhaps the picketers sensed how desperate the strikebreakers had been to accept a job under such circumstances and how trapped the men now felt. A few union members did hurl insults and even spit at the men. The scene could have turned violent at that point, if the despised ones had replied in kind. This was a case in which not only "a soft answer turns away wrath," but when *no* answer is best! Surely God was present in the situation, restraining both sides—the strikers from violently attacking the men who wronged them, and Tom and his coworkers from saying or doing anything to inflame passions any further. The promise of Christ to the merciful is once again borne out. Those who give mercy, receive mercy.

For Further Reflection

1. Have you been so desperate at some point in your life that, like Tom in the film, you did something distasteful in order to survive or cope? How did you feel at the time? How did you resolve your feelings and the situation?

2. Even though no religious language is used in the scene, how and where is God a part of it, just as much as in such scenes as in the burning bush in *The Ten Commandments*?

3. How has the Creator been present at special times and events in your life? Were you aware of this at the time, or was this something you realized afterward, when you had more time to reflect upon it?

4. What is there within us that enables us to connect with another and grant mercy rather than revenge? Does our society support this, or is getting even valued more than mercy? How is Jesus' beatitude similar to "As you sow, so shall you reap"?

5. When and how in your life have you either granted or received mercy? Are there still unresolved differences or inflicted wrongs that a measure of mercy might restore?

HYMN: "God of Compassion, in Mercy Befriend Us" or "There's a Wideness in God's Mercy"

A Prayer

Gracious and merciful God, you created us for close fellowship, but we have turned away from you and your way to follow our own willful desires. Still, you bestow mercy upon us, calling us back even as you called to our unfaithful ancestors through the prophets. You went to the extremity of sending your Son to die on a cross that we might finally hear your call and return to your side. As we have received mercy through Christ's sacrificial death and glorious resurrection, help us also to be merciful to those who wrong us. Enable us to become conveyers of your grace, as, inspired by the vision of writers and filmmakers, we see you at work beyond the sacred page of Scripture. In Jesus' name we pray. Amen.

21. She Stoops to Conquer
Out of Africa

The LORD sets the prisoners free;
    the LORD opens the eyes of the blind.
The LORD lifts up those who are bowed down;
    the LORD loves the righteous.
The LORD watches over the strangers;

he upholds the orphan and the widow,
but the way of the wicked he brings to ruin.

Psalm 146:7b–9

Then Jesus told them a parable about their need to pray always and not to lose heart. He said, "In a certain city there was a judge who neither feared God nor had respect for people. In that city there was a widow who kept coming to him and saying, 'Grant me justice against my opponent.' For a while he refused; but later he said to himself, 'Though I have no fear of God and no respect for anyone, yet because this widow keeps bothering me, I will grant her justice, so that she may not wear me out by continually coming.'"

Luke 18:1–5

Let each of you look not to your own interests, but to the interests of others. Let the same mind be in you that was in Christ Jesus,

> who, though he was in the form of God,
>> did not regard equality with God
>> as something to be exploited,
> but emptied himself,
>> taking the form of a slave,
>> being born in human likeness.

Philippians 2:4–7a

Introduction

Karen Blixen came to Kenya a few years before the First World War seeking freedom from the patriarchal society of her native Denmark. Entering into a marriage of convenience in order to buy a plantation in the British colony, she is soon abandoned by her bon-vivant husband and thus is forced to run the coffee plantation by herself. During the years, she struggles with the forces of nature, often working in the fields with her native laborers. She becomes very concerned for the small tribe of Kikuyu living on her land. Her friendship with white hunter Denys Finch Hatton develops into a love affair, but he refuses to enter into what he regards as the conventional restraints of marriage. After several years of adventure and toil, a series of calamities of nature and health bankrupts Karen, forcing her to auction off her possessions and sell the plantation and return to Denmark. She is very worried about "her" Kikuyu. She has grown fond of the old chief and his tribe over the years, and thus cannot just walk away from them. What will happen to them when a new owner moves into the plantation house?

The Scene

In a montage sequence, we see Karen meeting with a series of colonial officials, but none of them can offer any help for the tribe. She refuses to accept "No," so she appeals to the next level. At the last office, where she is also turned down, she becomes aware that the new Governor is having a lawn reception and that she will be invited.

Karen eventually finds herself in the long receiving line, where she awaits her turn to greet the official and his wife. The Governor gives a nod of recognition when Karen is introduced. He tries to brush off her request for assistance in the matter of the Kikuyu, but she will not be denied. This is her last opportunity to help the tribe. Against all the rules of protocol, Karen kneels down on the grass and implores the official's

help. The Governor looks around as if seeking someone to extricate him from this embarrassing situation.
His aide is about to make Karen rise when Denys
arrives and tells them to wait, to listen to her. Karen
pleads her case, and the Governor gives a general reply
that he will look into the matter. "Do I have your
word?" Karen half asks, half demands. "You have
mine," the Governor's kindly wife interjects. The
Governor looks at her. That is enough for Karen. She
rises and shakes hands with her kindly benefactor, who
tells her that she regrets that they will not get to know
each other.

Reflection on the Scene

What Karen did at the Governor's reception "just isn't
done" in polite British society. But Karen desperately
cared for the little tribe. She knew all too well of the
harsh view and treatment of the natives by most white
colonialists. Like the widow in Jesus' parable, Karen
persisted until she found her way. A desperate situation
called for desperate measures. As in the Philippian
passage, Karen "emptied herself" of her dignity.
People just did not do what she did in polite society.
Bad form, you know. But she did, and she succeeded.
There were those in the colony who respected and
honored her for such concern and courage.

There is a wonderful scene near the end of the film as
Karen is leaving. She passes through the local club,
where she had been summarily ushered out of the gen-
tleman's bar when she had first arrived and sought a
drink. As she is passing by it for the last time, the men
invite her into the forbidden territory for a drink. She is
served, and the men stand and toast her. It is a tribute
that means more to her than any royal honor ever could.

So in our own lives it is those times when we forget ourselves for the sake of others, when we stoop from our high places and kneel on the grass, that we rise to the heights to which we are called. Calvin Laufer's hymn "Christ of the Upward Way" describes the paths of service well, declaring that it is while serving Christ that we truly are free. Karen is leaving Africa a seeming failure, but in the eyes of God and of her former neighbors she is a shining success, very rich in terms of service.

For Further Reflection

1. What causes or people have called you to forget yourself and your own needs? How did you feel while so engaged? Was it an important leadership role or a less glamorous one?

2. What obstacles did you meet? (Remember the church scene in *Entertaining Angels* in which Dorothy Day, looking up at a crucifix, pours out her frustration to Christ about such obstacles? See Meditation 11.) Did you persist, as Karen did? Or did they overcome you? How is persistence in an endeavor just as important as talent?

3. Where are there people and places that call to you now for help? What talent, time, or treasure do you have that could make life better for others? What are you waiting for?

4. How is Karen the embodiment of what the Psalmist declares in Psalm 146? How has she "set the prisoners free," "opened the eyes of the blind," and "lifted up those who are bowed down"? How is she what Martin Luther would call "a little Christ"?

Hymn: "Christ of the Upward Way" or "Come, Thou Long Expected Jesus"

A Prayer

Dear God, you call us "to blazoned heights and down the slopes of need." We thank you for the examples of people like Karen who persisted in their struggle to be of service. Even without invoking your name or knowing that whatever she did to "the least of these" she was doing it to you, she struggled to do the right thing. Help us, who claim to know you, to do as well. Open our eyes to those places and persons to which and to whom you call us. We ask this in the name of the One who came, not to be served, but to serve, Jesus the Christ. Amen.

22. The Grace of a Personality
Beautiful Dreamers

Vindicate me, O Lord,
    for I have walked in my integrity,
    and I have trusted in the Lord without
      wavering.
Prove me, O Lord, and try me;
    test my heart and mind.
For your steadfast love is before my eyes,
    and I walk in faithfulness to you.

Psalm 26:1–3

"Not everyone who says to me, 'Lord, Lord,' will enter the kingdom of heaven, but only the one who does the will of my Father in heaven. On

that day many will say to me, 'Lord, Lord, did we
not prophesy in your name, and cast out demons
in your name, and do many deeds of power in
your name?' Then I will declare to them, 'I never
knew you; go away from me, you evil doers.'"

Matthew 7:21–23

Introduction

The beautiful dreamers of the title are the American
poet Walt Whitman and Canadian psychiatrist
Maurice Bucke. This gem of a 1992 Canadian film
directed by John Kent Harrison celebrates the liberating friendship of the older and the younger man. (Later
Dr. Bucke became the first biographer of the poet.) The
two meet at a medical convention in Philadelphia and
immediately take a liking to each other. The poet
agrees to return with Dr. Bucke to his London,
Ontario, asylum to help him institute reforms for more
humane treatment of the mentally ill. During the ensuing summer months, the poet's spiritual power loosens
up the straight-laced doctor, brings his repressed wife
into a newfound discovery of self-worth and freedom,
and supports his friend against the prejudiced staff and
ignorant townspeople in his battle to treat the mentally
ill as human beings rather than animals.

The Scene

When Bucke and Whitman step off the train at
London, Ontario, they are greeted by the doctor's little
daughter, Birdie, and his wife, Jessie. Jessie is reserved,
not sure what to make of the disheveled-looking older
man or of the fact that her husband has traveled without his tie and is carrying, rather than wearing, his suit

coat. Little Birdie, with the instinct of a child, rushes to embrace the poet as well as her father.

Also on hand is Wallace, the flippant editor of the local newspaper. He asks for an interview with the poet. Dr. Bucke tries to say no, but Whitman readily agrees. "Fire away," he tells the reporter. Wallace, perhaps baiting the famous poet for a juicy quote, says that he has heard that Whitman is an atheist and is against the church. "Do you believe in the Bible?" Wallace asks Whitman. If he was fishing for a lively quotation, Wallace surely gets it, for the poet replies without hesitation, "Sure do. It seems that Jesus and the church got a divorce. . . . I don't believe that the God we believe in is a petty tyrant!"

Later we meet the local representative of the church, the Reverend Randall, a hidebound rector who warns his congregation that there is a new, modern threat to the church abroad, and that he is right in their midst. Both Walt and his friend are sitting in the congregation. The good Reverend is, of course, also against Dr. Bucke's attempt to reform the treatment of the patients at the asylum.

Reflection on the Scene

Too often Christ's worst enemies seem to be uncomprehending or uncaring leaders of the church. From the Pharisees of Jesus' day to the Grand Inquisitor of *The Brothers Karamazov* to the society-obsessed churches that Dorothy Day rejected in her student days, the church sometimes has followed ways that run counter to God's. Poet Walt Whitman's unorthodox faith and lifestyle were seen as a threat to the upholders of the status quo; yet the poet, like the Psalmist, "walked in my integrity," trusting in the God who was far bigger than many of the churchmen of his day could comprehend.

In reflecting upon your own church and your role in it, you might compare it to what you see in the two ways of walking with God represented by the poet and the clergyman of the film. Those of us in the church may bristle at Whitman's statement that the church and Jesus got a divorce, yet there is precedent for such a statement in the writings of the prophet Hosea. Certainly such a charge should make us think of and look at any way in which our churches might be behaving that is just the opposite of Jesus' intentions. We must remember what one theologian pointed out so well when he stated that the church is the one institution that exists primarily for those who are outside of it. The church is but an instrument of God for bringing the story of God's immeasurable love to the whole world.

For Further Reflection

1. Do you see any of the Reverend Randall's intolerance or fear in yourself or your church? How is the poet perhaps doing more of Christ's work than the Reverend?

2. Would Walt Whitman be welcomed and feel at home in your church? (His homosexuality is not dealt with in the film, other than an oblique reference to his not being married.) Would a poorly dressed person be accepted at a Sunday service?

3. How joyful is your lifestyle and that of your church? What communicates this joy? The greeters and people? The music? The architecture and sanctuary furnishings? Are children accepted at worship, even if they are noisy at times?

4. Earlier the poet had summed up his creed for Maurice: "All a man's got to do is to love the earth and sun. Don't argue about God. Take care of the weak and the stupid." How does the latter part fit in with Christ's teachings about loving neighbors? What are you or your church doing about this?

5. How can you best express the joy that Christ and poets such as Walt Whitman seek to bring to your life? The apostle Paul declared that the Corinthians were his living epistle. In what ways might you be an open letter for others to "read" about Christ? What would a stranger "read" if she came to your church? Where is joy and liberation expressed in your worship liturgy? In the way strangers are welcomed? In the way children are accepted and celebrated?

6. If you have a copy, read out loud selections from Walt Whitman's *Leaves of Grass*. What non-Christians do you know who might be doing Christ's work as surely as church members are?

HYMN: "Joyful, Joyful We Adore Thee" or "I Danced in the Morning"

A Prayer

Dear God, you danced and sang at creation, and have sent poets and artists to help us to join in the music. We thank you for the insights of artists, of filmmakers and others who call us to celebrate your goodness ever more joyfully, and thus faithfully. Help us to walk in integrity and to do the will of your Son, that we might know the liberation that Christ brings. Make us an open book to others so that they too will want to turn to the Author. We ask this in the name of the original Beautiful Dreamer, Jesus Christ, our Lord. Amen.

23. Cheap Grace and Costly Grace
The Mission

Bless the LORD, O my soul,
    and all that is within me,
    bless his holy name.
Bless the LORD, O my soul,
    and do not forget all his benefits—
who forgives all your iniquity,
    who heals all your diseases,
who redeems your life from the Pit,
    who crowns you with steadfast love and mercy,
who satisfies you with good as long as you live,
    so that your youth is renewed like the eagle's.

                                      Psalm 103:1–5

And I said: "Woe is me! I am lost, for I am a man of unclean lips, and I live among a people of unclean lips; yet my eyes have seen the King, the LORD of hosts!"

    Then one of the seraphs flew to me, holding a live coal that had been taken from the altar with a pair of tongs. The seraph touched my mouth with it and said, "Now that this has touched your lips, your guilt has departed and your sin is blotted out."

                                        Isaiah 6:5–7

"Come to me, all you that are weary and are carrying heavy burdens, and I will give you rest."

                                      Matthew 11:28

For this is the message you have heard from the beginning, that we should love one another. We must not be like Cain who was from the evil one and murdered his brother.

                                      1 John 3:11–12a

Introduction

The Mission is the story of the spiritual journey of two men in eighteenth-century South America. Rodriguez is a rough soldier of fortune engaged in raiding and enslaving the natives living in the jungles near the Spanish and Portuguese border settlements. Father Gabriel is the gentle head of the Jesuit mission to the Guarani people located upriver, beyond the great falls that form a natural barrier dividing mission lands from the settlements. Their story becomes embroiled in the power politics of the time, the Spanish and Portuguese settlers plotting to have the mission lands transferred to Portuguese jurisdiction because Portuguese law permits the enslavement of indigenous people.

Rodriguez has a lover, but while he is away on his raids she has become attracted to Rodriguez's younger brother, Filipe. One fateful day Rodriguez returns early from his foray and catches the two lovers together. He is so enraged that he takes after his brother with his sword. Filipe pleads and tries to reason with him, but the soldier will not listen. Blinded by hurt feelings and a sense of betrayal, Rodriguez continues to attack. The brother puts up a feeble defense that is no match for Rodriguez's skill. He runs Filipe through with his blade.

The Scene

Rodriguez is sitting alone in his prison cell when Father Gabriel comes to him. The priest's words so arouse Rodriguez's anger that he grabs the cleric by the collar and forces him up against the wall. Father Gabriel is not afraid, continuing to speak calmly. Rodriguez says there is no hope for him, no way out.

There is a way out, Father Gabriel asserts, if the soldier dares to try. Rising to the challenge, Rodriguez fires back, If you dare to fail.

A small party of missioners led by Father Gabriel comes to the base of the huge cliff by the great falls. Rodriguez, now clad in a ragged brown robe like the brothers, lags behind them. He is dragging a heavy bundle in a huge net. It clangs and clatters over the rocks, and we see that the burden consists of his armor and weapons. As the men climb slowly up the wet rocks and then the sheer face of the mountain, Rodriguez's burden snags and sometimes causes him to fall back. He loses his footing and slips and slides downward for a considerable distance before stopping. As time passes, the other missioners, Brother John in particular, ask Father Gabriel to allow Rodriguez to let go of his burden. He's done enough penance, the younger priest asserts. Father Gabriel replies that that is for Rodriguez to say. And so the ex-soldier continues to stumble and stagger under his burden. Brother John grows so upset that he cuts the rope, and the packet falls into a gully. Far from looking relieved, Rodriguez laboriously climbs back down the cliff, reties the rope, and painfully hauls it up to where the party is resting.

Finally, after days of slow, painful climbing, the party reaches the top. They are spotted, and soon the Guarani mission people arrive to welcome them. They stop when they see Rodriguez. He is all too well known to the indigenous tribes of the area. A missioner takes a knife and rushes over to the ex-soldier, who is seated, exhausted, on the ground. Holding the knife to the white man's throat, he looks to the chief—and then cuts the rope and hurls Rodriguez's burden over the edge of the cliff. With a loud clanging and clattering sound it tumbles into the river far below. Rodriguez makes no move to retrieve it this time. Great tears fall from his eyes as his body is wracked with his sobbing. The Guarani laugh, and Father Gabriel embraces the repentant sinner. Letting him cry on his shoulder, the priest holds him in a grace hug.

Reflection on the Scene

"Amazing grace, how sweet the sound," wrote an ex-slave-ship captain at about the same time as the story of Father Gabriel and Rodriguez takes place. Rodriguez, who saw no way out of the horrible guilt of slaying his own brother, had not counted on what the wiser Father Gabriel knew—the amazing grace of God. And so, when the Guarani used his knife to cut him free from his burden rather than to slit his throat in vengeance, the hardened ex-soldier breaks down and cries. But his are tears of joy, even as the laughter of those who had once been his victims and enemies also is of joy. He knows that he was lost, but now is found.

Brother John's cutting of the rope earlier was an act that German theologian Dietrich Bonhoeffer would call "cheap grace." Grace without a cross, grace that did not take into account the full measure of the past sin of Rodriguez. Father Gabriel knew this, and so did Rodriguez himself. The mistaken pity of the younger priest would not have brought the release that only true grace could bring—the unexpected forgiveness of the Guarani of the man who had so wronged them. When we see the Guarani rush to Rodriguez and hold his knife poised at the white man's throat, we almost expect him to slit it. Before the love of Christ visited them, the tribesman would have killed his enemy. But through Father Gabriel and the missioners' preaching and teaching of the gospel, he had received grace, and now it flows through him to the man so desperately in need of it.

Rodriguez was like Isaiah, aware that he was a "man of unclean lips" and more, for he was like Cain, who murdered his own brother. The Guarani were the only ones who—like the seraph in the temple taking the tong and touching the prophet's lips with a live coal—were in a position to free their former oppressor from his guilt. By forgiving him for his sin against their people, they were also freeing him from his sin against his slain brother. The scene of the soldier sobbing in the arms of the priest is one of the most beautiful moments of grace recorded on film.

Few of us plunge so deeply into the depths of depravity as did Rodriguez, and yet we all stand in need of the same grace. This is exactly what the Scriptures promise us, that God's love is so great that he "forgives all your iniquity" and "heals all your diseases." The cross on which Christ died reveals both the depth of our human sin and the depth of divine love. When we have hurt others, when we have made a mess of our relationships with family or friends so that we feel like we are in the Psalmist's pit with no way out, may this film remind us of the gospel truth that in Christ, all is forgiven.

For Further Reflection

1. How would you feel if you were Rodriguez and had just killed your brother? How is the penance assigned him by Father Gabriel appropriate? Can you think of other creative ways in which our penance could be acted out? Think of such sins as lying to someone; smearing the character of a coworker

through gossip; stealing. Why is finding a way to act out penance more helpful than just praying and asking for forgiveness?

2. What in your life seems to burden or entangle you? What will it take to be free of it?

3. Where do you see examples of "cheap grace" in contemporary society? A TV evangelist confessing tearfully to the sin of adultery but then refusing to submit to the discipline of his denomination because he would be required to give up his lucrative TV ministry for a time? A politician tearfully expressing sorrow after his lies are exposed but not apologizing to the women whom he has used over the years?

4. Who has, like Father Gabriel, administered tough love to you when you had gone astray? To whom have you had to administer tough love?

Hymn: "Amazing Grace" or "Goin' to Lay My Burden Down"

A Prayer

Dear God, what a mess we make of our lives at times! We know what is right, for we have heard and read your word so many times—at church and in our Bible reading at home. How we pretend to others that nothing is wrong! We become so adept at covering up; thus we increase our original sin until it becomes like a heavy burden weighing us down. But we know that there is a way out, because your Son, who called himself "the way, the truth, and the life," invites "all those who are heavy laden" to come unto him. Help us to accept his invitation, for we know it is one that leads to joyful living, freed from the burdens of the past and open to the joy and challenge of the future. Amen.

24. No Greater Love
The Deer Hunter

Guard me as the apple of the eye;
   hide me in the shadow of your wings,
from the wicked who despoil me,
   my deadly enemies who surround me.
They close their hearts to pity;
   with their mouths they speak arrogantly.

Psalm 17:8–10

No one has greater love than this, to lay down
one's life for one's friends.

John 15:13

Beloved, let us love one another, because love is
from God; everyone who loves is born of God
and knows God.

1 John 4:7

Introduction

The Deer Hunter is the story of how three hunting and
drinking buddies and their friends are affected by the
Vietnam War. Michael, Nick, and Steven have been
called up to service, but before they leave they go hunting in the western Pennsylvania mountains one last
time together and attend Steven's wedding. In Vietnam
their idealism is shattered by the brutal fighting.
Captured by the Vietcong, they are forced to play a
harrowing game of Russian roulette. Michael manages
to trick their captors, shooting several of them and
then escaping with his two friends. But one of them is
injured, and during the grueling flight through the
jungle, the three are separated. Michael is rescued by

helicopter and returned to the United States. He visits Steven in a hospital, where he learns that his friend has been receiving money from an anonymous source in Saigon. Nick, of course, is the source of the money. He had awakened in a Saigon hospital deeply disturbed and confused by the terrible ordeal of their captivity. Too sick in heart and head to go home, Nick had fallen into the dissolute life centered around the gambling dens of Saigon. Michael flies to South Vietnam's capital during the last days when the American forces are pulling out. With the help of a guide, he finally locates Nick in a sleazy gambling den where the customers find excitement by betting on one of two men playing Russian roulette.

The Scene

Nick is one of the regulars who have survived many nights of playing the deadly game. It is the winnings from his risky pursuit that he has been sending back to Steven in the stateside hospital. But Nick does not seem to recognize Michael. He seems almost catatonic when his friend tries to remind him of their past together. Michael tells him that he loves him, but Nick's reply is to spit in his face. He returns to the game room. Knowing that time is short, Michael hastily bribes the owner to allow him to join in the game. It is the only way at the moment that he can sit down with Nick.

Michael takes his place across the table facing his friend. As the noisy crowd places its bets, he tries to talk with Nick, telling him that they do not have much time. Nick raises the gun, loaded with one bullet, and points it at his own head. "Don't do it!" Michael shouts. Nick pulls the trigger, and we hear the sound of the hammer striking an empty chamber. Now it is

Michael's turn. He picks up the gun as he asks, "Is this what you want?" He points the muzzle at his head. "I love you," he says, and then pulls the trigger. Another empty sound. The crowd's blood-lust increases—just four chambers to go. Nick picks up the gun again. Michael continues to plead, "Come on, Nicky. Come home. Just come home!" He tries to awaken some memory in his friend, some connection between them hidden somewhere in the darkened recesses of the mind of the zombielike creature before him. Nick points the gun and pulls the trigger. A loud explosion fills the room. Blood spurts from Nick's head. Michael screams in horror as he rushes to Nick. He cradles his friend's head in his arms and sobs.

Reflection on the Scene

The Deer Hunter forcefully reminds us that those who fall on the field of battle are not the only casualties of war. Soldiers like Nick, traumatized by the horrors of battle and captivity, strung out by drugs used to dull pain and to escape haunting memories, are also casualties, the walking dead. Michael learns the hard lesson that sometimes not even love is enough. His love for his friend ran so deep that he was willing to track him down in a far corner of the world and risk his own life in order to reach him. The crowd in the gambling den could have been those described by the Psalmist, so "closed to pity" were they. And yet Michael was like the one held up by Jesus to his disciples, willing to lay down his life for his friend. But none of this registered on Nick's consciousness. He had fallen too far to be called back.

Michael returns to the United States wounded in spirit yet resilient enough, as we see in subsequent scenes, to affirm the goodness of life and to enter into it once more. Perhaps it is because a love very much like that exhibited by a rabbi to his friends long before continues to abide in him. Love might not have been able to save Nick, but it does revive Michael, and through him will enrich the lives of his friends. We are not shown much in the film of Michael's spiritual life—there is a scene set in an Orthodox Church, but it is of Steven's lavish wedding. But whether or not he is a practicing believer, Michael's sacrificial love for his friend is surely, in the author of First John's words, "of God."

For Further Reflection

1. How is Michael's love like that of Christ? Do you see any significance in the name Michael? How is Michael like an angel for his friends?

2. What similarities in this film do you see to the stories of the Prodigal Sons and the Loving Father? What differences do you see? For instance, does Michael wait for Nick's return from the "far country"? (In this respect, perhaps he is more like the shepherd in the parable also found in Luke 15.)

3. Michael and Nick's situation, of course, is extreme. Where or when have you seen sacrificial love? How is parental love often like this?

4. For whom would you be willing to lay down your life? If you can think of more than one person, make a list. Think about what there is about them for which you would make such a sacrifice. Who do you think might make such a sacrifice for you?

5. What difference does it make in your life knowing that there are those for whom you would die, and who would die for you? We are reminded often by the

apostle Paul that Christ sacrificed his life for us. What difference does this make? What does it reveal to us about the love of God? How are you living up to the kind of love and expectation God has for you?

HYMN: "What Wondrous Love Is This?" or "They'll Know We Are Christians by Our Love"

A Prayer

Gracious and loving God, you love us with a love deeper than the ocean, higher than the heavens, and wider than the horizon. Even when we flee far from you, you search us out and, through the death of your Son on the cross, show us how far you are willing to go to bring us back home. Fill us with your loving Spirit so that we, too, like Michael in our story, will be able to go out in love to others, accepting and supporting them, even as you accept and support us. Through Jesus Christ, the Lord of Love, we pray. Amen.

25. Like a Child
To Kill a Mockingbird

Happy are those who consider the poor;
    the LORD delivers them in the day of trouble.
The LORD protects them and keeps them alive;
    they are called happy in the land.

                                        Psalm 41:1

The wolf shall live with the lamb,
    the leopard shall lie down with the kid,
the calf and the lion and the fatling together,
    and a little child shall lead them.

                                        Isaiah 11:6

"Let the little children come to me, and do not stop them; for it is to such as these that the kingdom of heaven belongs."

Matthew 19:14

Introduction

Atticus Finch, a widower raising a small daughter and son, is a lawyer in a small Southern town. He is given the unpopular task of defending a black man accused of raping a white woman. This is not an expedient thing for him to do, given the white supremacy views of so many of the people of the area. When the sheriff has to go out of town, he asks Atticus to watch the jail for the night. He is concerned that a lynch mob might arise to take justice into their own hands.

The Scene

As the sheriff had feared, a mob of angry white farmers drives up that night in front of the courthouse. Meanwhile, Atticus's twelve-year-old son, Jem, and younger daughter, Scout, have missed their father at home, so they go out with a young friend to look for him. Seeing the mob gathered at the courthouse, they come closer for a better look. Atticus, a book in hand, has been sitting in front of the courthouse door. The children, unable to see much through the crowd of men, run up and join Atticus.

Upset and worried for their safety, the lawyer orders the children to leave, but Jem refuses. Angered now, Atticus raises his voice. A man grabs Jem and orders him to get going, but Scout kicks the man in the shin. "Ain't nobody gonna do Jem that-a-way," she says. Atticus continues to try to send the children away, but

Jem, knowing the danger his father is in, refuses. Scout looks around the crowd and recognizes a man.

"Hey, Mr. Cunningham . . ." The man, whom her father has been helping with a legal problem and whose son is a classmate of hers, looks uncomfortable at being singled out. Scout comes a bit closer to him: "Don't you remember me, Mr. Cunningham? I'm Jean Louise Finch. You brought us some hickory nuts early one morning, remember? We had a talk. I went and got my daddy to come out and thank you. I go to school with your boy. I go to school with Walter. He's a nice boy. Tell him 'hey' for me, won't you? You know something, Mr. Cunningham, entailments are bad. Entailments . . ."

The crowd has become strangely silent. Realizing now that all eyes were on her, Scout self-consciously breaks off and turns to her father, "Atticus, I was just sayin' to Mr. Cunningham that entailments were bad but not to worry. Takes a long time sometimes . . ." Again her words stop. She looks around, at her father and at the silent men. "What's the matter? I sure meant no harm, Mr. Cunningham."

"No harm taken, young lady." He comes up and, bending down to her level, holds her shoulders for a moment. "I'll tell Walter you said 'hey,' little lady." Straightening up, he waves his hand to the other men. "Let's clear outta here. Let's go, boys."

Reflections on the Scene

Scout has been blessed with a father who embodies the Psalmist's concern for the poor. Atticus takes on their legal cases for little more than a sack of hickory nuts and even accepts the thankless task of defending a black handyman in the old South. Scout has imbibed his color-blind principles, as we see in this scene, filled with the echoes of Isaiah and of Christ.

Unlike her older brother, she is too young and innocent to realize what the mob is intent on doing. In fact, she does not see a mob, but a gathering of farmers, one of whom she knows. By singling him out by name, the innocent little girl brings out his humanity, connecting with it through shared memories. He is Walter, not an anonymous member of a mob. As a faceless part of a mob, he is capable of killing, but not as Walter. Each would-be lyncher realizes this and comes to his senses, and thus a potentially tragic situation is completely defused. Even within each member of the mob there exists what Abraham Lincoln, in his eloquent plea to his divided nation not to separate, called "the better angels of our nature."

This powerful scene has much to teach us about the underlying humanity that all human beings share. There is a deep respect, even for people some would label as "crackers" or "rednecks," in Harper Lee's work that often is not found in other accounts of Southern whites. For example, in both *Mississippi Burning* and *A Time to Kill*, white segregationists are portrayed as subhumans who deserve to suffer and die. In fact, in the first film, when a white deputy sheriff is threatened with castration unless he tells the FBI agents where the bodies of the three missing civil rights workers are buried, the theater audience cheered! That's a long way from the situation in *To Kill a Mockingbird*. There are indeed times when we need a little child to lead us, as in Isaiah's prophecy, a child whose unprejudiced vision of a kingdom where warring beasts (and humans) dwell together in peace, a kingdom known to Jesus as "the kingdom of heaven."

For Further Reflection

1. How difficult is it for you to see the humanity within someone whose views or actions you strongly disapprove of? Have you ever thought it strange or ironic that those who claim to promote love and justice for minorities often are very intolerant of those they regard as bigots and racists?

2. How can our faith both help and hinder our connecting with the humanity in those we despise? (See Psalm 139:19–22 for an example of the former; for the latter, look at the way Jesus treated the despised and the way he reacted to his tormentors at his crucifixion.)

3. How has a child shown some insight or gem of wisdom in your life? How has a child's mere presence helped soften a tense situation? For an example of the latter, consider tired, bored adults who are sitting in a doctor's office, with little interaction among them. Someone comes in with an infant or toddler. What often happens?

4. What do you think are the childlike qualities that Jesus seemed to treasure and desire for his followers?

5. How are race relations in your community? What are the churches doing to improve them? How and where are you, or could you be, involved? How could "a little child" lead you toward fulfilling Isaiah's vision, what Martin Luther King Jr. called "the beloved community"? Can the children of the church schools and/or the public schools be involved in some way?

HYMN: "Lord, I Want to Be a Christian"

A Prayer

Dear God, who has made of one blood all peoples and nations, continue to mold us after the pattern of

Christ, that we might see everyone as created in your image, even the most debased of humans whose deeds or views we abhor. May we dream, and may we live the ancient dream of a "beloved community" where all peoples, and even all creatures, dwell together in harmony and security. We ask this in the name of your Son, who died praying even for his enemies. Amen.

26. Any Sign of Change?
Tender Mercies

Have mercy on me, O God, according to thy
   steadfast love;
     according to thy abundant mercy blot out my
      transgressions.
Wash me thoroughly from my iniquity, and
   cleanse me from my sin!

                 Psalm 51:1–2 (RSV)

How can we who died to sin still live in it? Do you not know that all of us who have been baptized into Christ Jesus were baptized into his death? We were buried therefore with him by baptism into death, so that as Christ was raised from the dead by the glory of the Father, we too might walk in newness of life.

                 Romans 6:2b–4 (RSV)

For the word of the cross is folly to those who are perishing, but to us who are being saved it is the power of God.

              1 Corinthians 1:18 (RSV)

Introduction

Mac Sledge, once a famous country-western singer and songwriter, takes to the bottle after his divorce from his singer wife, Dixie. After days of drinking and sleeping it off, he wakes up in a motel room alone. His friends have all run off. He offers to work off his motel bill. Single mother Rosa Lee, owner of the motel, needs the help, so she agrees. The relationship with her and her young son, Sonny, starts off slowly, but Mac's work and determination not to drink again apparently win her admiration and then her heart. We are not shown much of the growing romance, just the results—they marry. Mac accompanies Sonny and Rosa Lee to church where she sings in the choir and Sonny is planning to be baptized. When the friendly pastor meets Mac and learns that he has not been baptized, he says, "We'll have to work on that." Although we never see the process, the preacher evidently acted on his words.

The Scene

In church we see Rosa Lee singing with the choir. They finish their anthem, and then it is time for Sonny's baptism. The curtains part, and the pastor baptizes Sonny by immersion in the name of the Trinity. Rosa Lee looks on with a mother's love, pride, and quiet joy. The curtains close, and then unexpectedly open again. Mac is standing in the baptistery with the pastor. He too is baptized, as someone says "Amen."

Later, the three are in Mac's truck. Sonny keeps looking at himself in the rearview mirror during the following exchange: "Well, we've done it, Mac. We're baptized." Mac replies, "Yeah, we are." Sonny continues, "Everybody said I was going to feel like a changed person. I guess I do feel a little different, but I don't feel a whole lot different. Do you?" Mac, "Not yet." "You don't look different," Sonny says as he looks at Mac, "Do you think I look any different." Mac only answers with another, "Not yet."

Reflection on the Scene

Sonny is young and tends to take the observations of adults literally, hence his looking into the mirror and at Mac for signs of a visible change. He has not been through the soul-searing experiences of Mac, although he is trying to cope with the loss of his father, the taunts of some of his playmates, and his mother's marriage to the older Mac. On the other hand, Mac has come a long way in his spiritual life, from the heights of stardom, to the depths of divorce and alcoholism, back to the heights of his love for Rosa Lee and Sonny, and now to the spiritual renewal confirmed in his baptism. His reply of "Not yet" is important; it is not just an offhand remark. It shows that Mac possesses a deep understanding of faith and conversion as an ongoing process, not just a once-for-all-time, miraculous event.

In Paul's two Corinthian letters, the Greek word for "saved" is properly translated in the RSV and NRSV texts as "being saved" (1 Cor. 1:18 and 2 Cor. 2:15), rather than simply "saved," as in the KJV. Both Mac and the apostle Paul see salvation as taking place over a period of time, a lifetime for most of us. Mac will know both success and disappointment, even intense grief, before the film is over. Indeed, he will question the ways of the world and of God, but because of what he did, and what was done for him, in that little church, and because of his love for his new family, Mac will continue to grow spiritually, building upon the solid foundation of his new faith, of which his baptism is but an outward symbol.

For Further Reflection

1. In their church tradition of "believer's baptism," Sonny and Mac will always be able to look back and remember the experience. Can you remember your baptism, or were you baptized as an infant? If so, did your parents or church leaders tell you anything about the event? How did your church or family help you to understand and accept your baptism? Was your confirmation an experience of growth and understanding, and finally, of conscious acceptance of Christ?

2. Have you seen the poster in which we see the girders of a building under construction with the slogan, "Be patient with me. God is not finished with me yet"? How is this an amplification of Mac's "Not yet" and of the apostle Paul's "being saved"? Of salvation as being not a done deal, but a continuing negotiation?

3. What has contributed to your spiritual development? The church? Your friends and family? The events in your life? How have tragic or bad experiences, such as those in *Tender Mercies*—Mac's divorce and fall from success, his drinking, and the death of his only daughter—contributed to your faith journey? In fact, would your faith have been so strong or resilient without the bad or difficult events of life?

4. The reformer Martin Luther at times felt so pressured by the charges of heresy against him by the official church and its attempts to destroy him that he almost broke down. Then he would repeat the Latin form of "I have been baptized! I have been baptized!" How can such knowledge—that the church placed water on you

in the name of the Triune God and declared that you are a child of the covenant—be a saving factor during times of stress? Can such knowledge be a means of grace, as the sacrament is called, by giving you a sense of identity, of knowing who and Whose you are?

5. Look up your church's baptismal liturgy and prayerfully read through it again. At what points does it proclaim the goodness and love of God? Your own worth as a child of the covenant? Your place amid God's people? The next time there is a baptism in your congregation, use the ceremony as a means of renewing your own.

HYMN: "O for a Closer Walk with God" or "I Sing a Song of the Saints of God"

A Prayer

Dear and gracious God, you have called each of us into your covenant and showed by the visible symbol of water that we belong to you and not just to ourselves. Your Spirit that hovered over the waters at Creation and led the children of Israel through the waters of the Sea from slavery to freedom has washed over us as well and entered into our innermost being, proclaiming your acceptance of us in Christ. We have died to our old ways of self-centeredness and risen in newness of life in Christ. Still, the old ways tempt us as we try to follow in the paths in which you would lead us. Continue to strengthen us by the knowledge of our baptism, symbol of our acceptance, that we might remain loyal and steadfast. We pray this in the name of the One who died for us, Jesus Christ, our Lord. Amen.

27. Grace Returned
The Color Purple

How long, O LORD? Will you forget me forever?
   How long will you hide your face from me?
How long must I bear pain in my soul.,
   and have sorrow in my heart all day long?
How long shall my enemy be exalted over me?

Psalm 13:1–2

Send out your bread upon the waters,
   for after many days you will get it back.

Ecclesiastes 11:1

"Blessed are the meek, for they will inherit the earth."

Matthew 5:5

Introduction

No Charles Dickens character ever suffered as much as the victimized heroine in Steven Spielberg's adaptation of Alice Walker's novel. Spanning almost forty years, *The Color Purple* is the story of Celie, a black girl first abused by the man she calls "Pa." As soon as she has a child, Pa takes it and gives it away (or sells it), apparently not wanting to live with the fruit of his illicit lust. One day, "Mister" comes to bargain for Celie's sister, Nettie, but Pa refuses to part with her, selling him the less attractive Celie instead. Charming on the surface, Mister beats Celie once he has her home and refuses to support her in disputes she has with his unruly brood of children. She has a brief respite from her misery when Nettie comes to visit her. The two have always been the best of friends, romping through fields and woods together. Nettie tells her that she shouldn't let the children run over her, but Celie replies, "I don't know how to fight. All I know is how to survive." When Nettie resists Mister's attempt to rape her by kicking him in the groin, the angry man throws her off the farm, vowing never to allow her to have contact with Celie again. He keeps his vindictive vow by hiding all of Nettie's letters to her sister over the years.

Years pass, and Celie settles into the abused life of the meekest of the meek. Mister flaunts his relationship with his mistress Shug, an alcoholic juke joint singer. Celie raises no objections, merely doing what she does best—surviving. Her husband's is a graceless world of the strong lording it over the weak, but grace does enter Celie's world through two women. In the end Christ's promise that "the meek shall inherit the earth" finally comes true for Celie. In this meditation we focus on the first of these women bearers of grace— Sofia.

The Scenes

When we first see her, Sofia is a big woman bossing a grown-up Harpo, Mister's oldest son, as Harpo brings her home to meet his father. She is in "a family way." Mister, wanting no part of such a wild female, refuses to bless them or give Harpo permission to marry, but the next scene shows us Sofia and Harpo being joined as husband and wife in church. Celie and Mister are in the congregation. There follows a series of short scenes in which Sofia dominates the hapless Harpo. He asks his father, and even Celie, what he should do. Mister tells him he must beat Sofia in order to show her who is boss. Surprisingly, Celie echoes this advice. Sofia, her face bruised, angrily confronts Celie, demanding to know why she told Harpo to beat her.

"All my life I've had to fight," she tells Celie. "I had to fight my daddy. I had to fight my uncle." Sofia tells Celie that she will kill Harpo before she gives in to him. Celie can only reply piously. "This life be over soon. Heaven lasts forever," an answer that will never satisfy Sofia, even though she is a preacher's daughter. Harpo and she continue to fight, Sofia giving as much as she receives in physical abuse. Finally, fed up, she packs up and leaves with their children.

Sometime later, Sofia is shopping in town when the Mayor's wife stops to admire Sofia's little ones. Repelled by the white woman's condescending airs, Sofia remains cold and distant. She turns down an offer from the family to become their maid, insulting the Mayor's wife in the process. When the Mayor slaps her, Sofia hits him back, just as she had returned Harpo's blows so many times. Clearly stepping across forbidden boundaries, Sofia is arrested on trumped-up charges and imprisoned, where she suffers such harsh and brutal treatment that her strong spirit is broken. She is finally released on condition that she serve as maid to the Mayor and his arrogant wife. Accompanying the Mayor's wife to the store, Sofia encounters Celie for the first time in years. The once proud woman now limps and cannot focus her eyes because of the beatings she has endured. Thus she stands helpless for a moment when the white woman gives her a list and tells her to gather the items on it. Celie steps forward. She is far more confident now, for she has been reading such Dickens novels as *Oliver Twist* during the intervening years. She takes the list from Sofia and gathers the items on it for her. When Sofia leaves with the white woman, she silently mouths "Thank you" to Celie.

Reflection on the Scene

Celie's time with Sofia is brief, and she is soon gone from Celie's life—for a while. Yet her impact on Celie remains, deeply impressed upon her memory. Other than her sister Nettie, Celie has never seen such a strong woman, able to stand up uncowed before a man and give as much as she takes in abuse. When Sofia does leave Harpo, it must have made quite an impact on Celie's mind, for this is an alternative that she herself has never thought of.

But we also see that such strong determination to stand up for one's rights can lead to trouble in a society based on a racist caste system. Sofia's crossing of the unyielding boundary separating the races is her undoing, for the Jim Crow system is able to exert such vicious pressure that it is able to break even her strong spirit. Although stronger at first than Celie, Sofia's strength is too rigid. Celie is more like a willow tree, bending in the wind; whereas Sofia is more like a brittle tree that resists for a while but, when the wind blows ever stronger, breaks.

In the scene in the store we see the operation of grace received now returned. Sofia had blessed Celie, and like "bread cast on the waters" it comes back to her in Celie's little act of kindness in the store. It is a lovely, little moment of grace that no one else there would have noticed. But for the dispirited and disabled Sofia, it was a precious moment. She still has more pain and disappointment to go through, but there will come a time when, for her and for Celie, "the meek will inherit" if not the earth, then at least some of their due—when the two women rise up at that wonderful meal near the end of the film and stand against their male oppressors.

For Further Reflection

1. How does the story of Celie help us to understand why a woman in an abusive relationship would stay with her husband? Given her limitations, what choice did she have? Who would have helped her? Before she met Sofia, where would Celie have gotten even the *idea* of resisting Pa or Mister?

2. In the novel, Celie writes a series of letters to God. How are these like the Psalmist's prayer? Where do you see God in her story? In Celie's very will to survive? In Sofia's example of defiance?

3. The author of Ecclesiastes poetically advises us to give, and we will receive. How is this similar to "As we sow, so shall we reap"? How is Celie's little act of kindness in the store an example of this? Do you think the writer meant us to "send out our bread" in a calculating or manipulative way? Or just to do random acts of kindness, heedless of the results?

4. How does Jesus' beatitude fly in the face of the values of society? What usually happens to the meek? If you know how the film and novel turn out, how is Jesus' promise vindicated? It has been suggested that the Greek word translated as "meek" could also be "gentle." How might this be a more appropriate translation?

5. How or where in your experience have you seen the Scripture passages borne out? How have your past wounds been healed? If you prayed, were your prayers answered when and in the way that you asked? Or did God answer in God's own time and way?

HYMN: "What a Friend We Have in Jesus"

A Prayer

Gracious God, like a great artist you have filled our world with colors so that maybe, as Alice Walker observes, you are a bit—well, upset—when we pass by a field of purple flowers and fail to appreciate them. We know that you are not only the God of beauty but of justice as well. You are on the side of the Celies and Sofias of this world, for you took up the cause of Israel in Egypt, and of the poor of Israel when their own kings oppressed them. Your Son tells us that as we act graciously "to the least," we do it for him. We pray for your forgiveness when we forget this. Grant that we might also be a part of your work of blessing the meek and the poor. Make us channels of your grace, even as we have been recipients of it when we were "the least of these." In the name of the compassionate Christ, your Son and our Lord, we pray. Amen.

28. Riding Grace
Pulp Fiction

Note: Few people think of Quentin Tarantino's Pulp Fiction *when they discuss spiritual themes in film. If you plan to use this meditation with a group, you need to warn them of the sordid conditions of the characters. This is definitely an R-rated film. The violence, drug use, and vulgar language make this unsuitable even for some adult groups, so proceed with caution.*

> Let not mercy and truth forsake thee: bind them about thy neck; write them upon the table of thine heart: So shalt thou find favour and good understanding in the sight of God and man.
>
> Proverbs 3:3–4 (KJV)

Do not rejoice when your enemies fall,
  and do not let your heart be glad when they
    stumble.

Proverbs 24:17

"Blessed are the merciful, for they will receive
mercy."

Matthew 5:7

Introduction

One of the most bizarre films to be included in this collection is the trendy film *Pulp Fiction*, so popular among young adults. What is surprising is that the theme of grace runs throughout the three interwoven stories. Whether intended by the filmmaker or not, the film declares that grace can be found in the most sordid of conditions, touching and in a couple of cases transforming the lives of the most depraved of peoples—in this case, two hit men; a conniving boxer and the mobster who has paid him to throw a big fight; and a nervous couple holding up a diner. We will concentrate on the story of the boxer in this meditation.

Butch Coolidge is a hard-hitting prizefighter who accepts a large sum of money from Marcellus Wallace, a mobster, to throw his next fight. It is a high-profile event with big money being laid down, mostly on the favored Butch to win. Because all the savvy fight fans are certain that Butch can easily take his opponent, Marcellus is able to find plenty of takers for his wagers against Butch. Thanks to Butch's dive, Marcellus will wind up even richer than he already is.

Butch, however, has other ideas, as we see during the events leading up to the fight. Not only is he proud of his boxing skills, but he sees his winning the fight as a way for him to win bets of his own, as well as the hefty payment by Marcellus, providing that he can quickly get away. He lays careful plans with his lover Fabienne to meet right away following the fight, with a minimum amount of luggage so they can flee quickly. He gives explicit instructions for Fabienne to bring his wristwatch with her. It is a family heirloom hidden by his father when he was a POW in North Vietnam.

The night of the fight arrives, and Butch meets his opponent in the ring. They go at it for several rounds, Butch clearly outclassing the hapless boxer. Then he hits the man so hard that he goes down, completely knocked out. The crowd breaks into a loud roar, and Butch hastens to his dressing room and then out the door. After meeting up with Fabienne at a motel, he discovers that in her hurry she had forgotten the coveted watch. Butch is furious, though he is gentle with her.

The Scene

Butch leaves Fabienne to return to his apartment for the watch. While driving back to the motel, however, Butch literally runs into the angry Marcellus. Marcellus gives chase to Butch through the streets. Barely ahead of his vengeful pursuer, Butch runs into a pawnshop, followed by Marcellus. The pawnbroker pulls a gun on the two and ties them up in a back room. He decides to have some fun with Marcellus in a room specially rigged for torturing. He leaves his somewhat dimwitted partner to guard Butch. Butch manages to free himself from his bonds, kill the captor, and run out of the shop.

About to take off to rejoin his lover, the fighter pauses for a moment, and then turns around and heads back to the shop. The bloodthirsty pawnbroker is having his way with Marcellus when Butch breaks into the room and kills the torturer. Butch warily unties Marcellus. The latter, relieved to be free and whole, tells Butch that the score is now even between them—but that he better leave town and never come back or fight in the ring again. Butch rejoins Fabienne, and they head for the airport on the motorcycle that Butch took from the pawnshop. The camera comes in for a close-up of the motorcycle. Painted on the side is the name of the bike: "Grace."

Reflection on the Scene

If you watched the movie before, did you notice the name of the motorcycle? Most people did not, but for those who did, the brief shot provided the clue for understanding the whole film. For some viewers, Tarantino's film is just a lurid, exciting thriller. But for those "with eyes that see, and ears that hear," the writer/director has provided a strange but meaningful visual parable. We do not know why Butch decided to turn back at the last moment to help the man bent on destroying him. Maybe his conscience was formed by his once having been a part of the church. Whatever it was, there is still a bit of decency in the heart of this avaricious fighter, enough to cause him to return and rescue Marcellus from a horrible fate. Butch's is an act of grace, though he himself is a long way from being a follower of the Galilean. Butch feels no remorse at brutally beating his rival in the ring, and he certainly does not regret killing the two sadists in the pawnshop.

In Butch's story there is little God-talk (unlike one of the other tales, that of the two hit men), and yet

God's grace is very much present in Butch's act of mercy. And the promise of Jesus' beatitude is fulfilled. As Butch had mercy on Marcellus, so the gangster responds in kind to the man who had just cheated him out of a fortune. Had Butch not returned to rescue Marcellus, he and Fabienne might have ridden away, but not to freedom. They would have stayed hidden in faraway countries for the rest of their lives to elude the vengeance of the mobster. Even if Marcellus had been killed by his captor, his successor would have continued to track down Butch. The mob could not afford to have someone cheat them and get away with it.

Probably no one who opens these pages will be in as extreme a condition as the denizens of *Pulp Fiction*. It is, after all, *pulp* fiction we are dealing with in this film, and yet it depicts the effects of grace or mercy as truthfully as any sermon or theological tome. Mercy begets mercy, or better, as Jesus put it, "Blessed are the merciful, for they will receive mercy." Many a tense situation in which one party is wronged by another could be defused if the injured person overlooked or forgave the hurt. Even Christians need to be reminded of this at times.

For Further Reflection

1. Were you a bit shocked by the claim that this film contained spiritual insights? Do you still have doubts about this? In that the film is so favored by young adults, why is it important that those in the church not write off the film?

2. The detail of the close-up revealing the name of the bike raises an old question of whether filmmakers are aware of the theological meaning in their films or

not. Sometimes, as in the case of Stuart Rosenberg's *Cool Hand Luke*, Robert Benton's *Places in the Heart*, or Horton Foote's scripts for *Tender Mercies* and *Trip to Bountiful*, they are very aware of this. What do you think about Quentin Tarantino? Even when the director and writer have no conscious religious or theological motives, is it not possible for believers to find themes of grace, sin and guilt, love and forgiveness in their films? Are not the Bible and theology about life in this world as much as in the next? Is God able to use the works of secular artists and filmmakers to reveal truths of ethics and the human spirit, as well as those produced by believers? (For biblical precedent, see Isaiah 10:5, wherein the prophet says that God is using the pagan Assyrians as the rod of his anger to punish Judah for its sins.)

3. Think back over your relationships: When did an act of forgiveness or mercy save the relationship? When did you see or experience a situation where these were not given? What happened to the relationship?

4. Think on the statement by Gandhi, often quoted by Martin Luther King Jr., that in a world that practices the ancient law of retribution, "an eye for an eye, and a tooth for a tooth," everyone will be blind.

5. Are there people you know who seem so lost in rapaciousness or other forms of sin that seemingly nothing can ever save them? What does the story of Butch and Marcellus say to this? A candidate for the ministry once surprised his examiners when he declared in his statement of faith that his concept of the kingdom of God included Adolph Hitler sitting down at a table with Anne Frank. What would you say to this person? Would such "amazing grace" be too radical?

6. In the hymn we sing that "there's a wideness in God's mercy, like the wideness of the sea." How wide is your mercy? What difference does this make in your life? At what points in your life have you experienced the "wideness in God's mercy"?

HYMN: "There's a Wideness in God's Mercy"

A Prayer

Loving God, your mercy is as wide as the cross, deeper than our sin, and as swift to be given as lightning. Beside you, we seem slow to forgive and to reconcile. We are quick to judge and blind to the possibilities of discovering your grace in others, especially in those whom we regard as morally inferior to ourselves. Help us to sing "Gracious Spirit, dwell with me, I myself would gracious be." We thank you for the insightful works of those who seek to entertain us, that sometimes even in the lurid, your piercing truth and amazing grace surprise us by their presence. May we continue to have "eyes that see and ears that hear" in our movie theaters as well as in our churches. In the name of the One whose gracious sacrifice on the cross has brought us into fellowship with you. Amen.

29. A Meal of Grace
Babette's Feast

Steadfast love and faithfulness will meet;
 righteousness and peace will kiss each other.
Faithfulness will spring up from the ground,
 and righteousness will look down from the sky.
Psalm 85:10–11

"Then people will come from east and west, from north and south, and will eat in the kingdom of God."

Luke 13:29

Put away from you all bitterness and wrath and anger and wrangling and slander, together with all malice, and be kind to one another, tenderhearted, forgiving one another, as God in Christ has forgiven you.

Ephesians 4:31–32

Introduction

Babette fled Paris during a time of brutal repression in the nineteenth century and found refuge in the home of two unmarried sisters ministering to the poor in their tiny village on the barren coast of Jutland. She serves as their live-in maid and cook, freeing the kindly sisters to spend more time with their parishioners. Their minister father had founded the ascetic Protestant community many years before, and his daughters each gave up a suitor and chose to stay and help in his ministry, carrying on even after his death. The people are delighted with Babette's presence, for they notice an immediate improvement in the food brought to them when she takes over the cooking chores from the sisters.

Many years pass, with Babette tending to the shopping and cooking while the sisters visit the aging residents with food and prayers. It will soon be the one hundredth anniversary of the birth of the community's founder, and the sect members are looking forward to a simple commemoration of the event. But all is not well spiritually with the little band of believers. Some carry grudges against each other, even though the hurt or slight happened years before. An old couple still live with the guilt that their love affair began while each was married to another, and they blame each other for their illicit acts. Sometimes, during the service held each week in the sisters' home, the people's hostility breaks forth so noticeably that Babette chastises the offenders when she serves them their refreshments.

Everyone is surprised when Babette receives a letter from France informing her that she has won ten thousand francs in the national lottery. Babette reveals to the sisters that her one tie to the old country had been the annual lottery ticket that a friend had bought for her during each of the past ten years. The sisters and villagers are even more surprised when Babette informs them that she would like to prepare a French meal in honor of the sect's founder. The people, being strictly ascetic, are not pleased, but they do not want to hurt Babette's feelings. They accept her offer, but they meet in private and pledge that they will take no notice of the food.

The Scene

The big night finally arrives, and so do the guests—not only the parish members, but a General Loewenhielm and his elderly aunt. A noblewoman, the aunt had been a benefactor of the community all during the time of the founder's pastorate. Her nephew had worshiped in the church many years before when, as a high-living young officer, he had been exiled by his father to live with the aunt for a period until he could mend his ways. While there he had met one of the daughters and been smitten with her, only to find his courage wilting under the stern and watchful eye of the Pastor. The shy officer left, never having been able to declare his love to her. Now, decades later, he is returning in triumph, expecting to parade his successful military career at the feast and show her what she missed.

The table set for the twelve is a glittering array of dishes, shining silverware, and a row of sparkling wine and water glasses for each diner. The sect members exchange glances and mutter quietly to each other that they will not take account of the food. The General is clearly taken aback by the sumptuous spread, the great quality of each dish and the rarity of the wines. He who had come to impress others is stirred to admiration for their unseen cook in this backwater village. In contrast, the simple church folk are enjoying the food despite themselves—and are totally oblivious to its high quality and cost. An elderly lady smacks her lips approvingly as she empties her wine glass and asks for more, declaring it good "lemonade." The cold reserve of the company slowly melts as Babette's fine cuisine works its magic, the latter enhanced by the General's running commentary on each dish.

The General rises and makes a short speech, a celebration of the marvelous grace believers enjoy. He declares that though it is thought to be limited, which makes us tremble out of fear of judgment, divine grace is actually infinite. Therefore we do not have to be afraid of making a wrong choice in life (and here he looks at the sister whom he had wanted to declare his love to long ago), that in the infinite divine mercy all choices and paths are brought together. The General closes by quoting the Pastor's favorite prayer, based on a verse from Psalm 85: "For mercy and truth have met together, and righteousness and bliss have kissed one another." During his little speech, the General and the sister whom he had longed for exchange meaningful looks. Each had taken very different paths, and yet, as the General tells her later as he is departing, in grace they have been together through the years. She quietly acknowledges this.

Grace is flowing into the lives of the sect members as well. Their palates tingling with the delicious food and their tongues loosened a bit by the many wines, they whisper words of reconciliation to each other. Two men forgive each other's cheating in a business deal, and the adulterous husband and wife come to terms with their past and with each other, kissing each other passionately for the first time in many years. Afterward, the departing guests go outside and sing as they dance in a circle. The stars in the heavens seem to the sisters to be much closer at that sacred moment.

Reflection on the Scene

Evidently something is transpiring at Babette's feast that is more than the ingesting of rich food and drink. In talking about the main course, the General describes a restaurant in Paris where he and his fellow officers loved to dine: such feasts were "a love affair of the noble and romantic category in which one no longer distinguishes between bodily and spiritual appetite or satiety." Babette is not a priest or minister (she calls herself an artist in a later scene), but her meal is a means of grace, just like the sacrament of Holy Communion. The only other film that celebrates the Eucharist as a means of grace in such a marvelous, memorable way is Robert Benton's *Places in the Heart.* Both films show warring parties, influenced by Word and sacrament, reaching out to one another in love and forgiveness. The words of the apostle Paul to the

Ephesians become a reality at the sisters' table, graced so beautifully by Babette's food, the sect members at last putting away "all bitterness and wrath and anger and wrangling and slander."

For some, the Eucharist is a routine ritual, but for those open to the movements of divine grace it can be an occasion of reconciliation and renewal. For Christians, the Eucharist—a spiritual meal dependent upon the physical, bread and wine—is the pattern for all meals, whether they be a simple breakfast or a sumptuous banquet. They are a time of sharing of more than just food, a time of coming together in love, a time of grace.

For Further Reflection

1. How have meals been important in your life? Were (or are) there times of sharing news of the day and engaging in discussion and games or songs? What are the special times when the whole family gathers to celebrate?

2. How is food important in the church? In the sacrament? At church suppers? When the community gathers following a funeral or a wedding? Think how all this parallels the stories of food in the Scriptures: Abraham entertaining the three angels; the observation of the Passover Meal; Elijah sojourning with the widow; Jesus at the wedding in Cana; the celebration marking the return of the younger son in the parable of the Waiting Father; the feeding of the multitudes; Jesus dining at the home of the tax collector Zacchaeus; the establishment of the Lord's Supper; the meal at Emmaus; the Easter breakfast by the Sea of Galilee. Where do you see grace in the above?

3. What was the most meaningful Communion service you can remember? What happened to make it so special? What was the most meaningful church/congregational meal for you?

4. There have often arisen in the church ascetic movements, such as the one founded by the Pastor in *Babette's Feast*. What gave rise to them? How do they often go too far in denying the excesses of those whom they rebel against? In the world that the author of Genesis 1 claims was created by and blessed as "good" by God, can there be a firm line separating the material and the spiritual? How do they impinge upon one another, as in this film?

5. Gandhi said something like "Bread eaten by oneself is physical, but bread shared with another is spiritual." What does this mean to you? Think on the meaning of the word *companion*, from the French meaning "sharer of the loaf."

HYMN: "I Come with Joy" or "O Bread of Life for All Men Broken"

A Prayer

God of grace, you blessed your creation, declaring it "good," and even "very good." We thank you for all of its wonder and beauty. We are grateful to you that even through our physical appetites your grace can enter our lives, transforming our outlook and relationships. We thank you for eyes to see, noses to smell, and taste buds to enjoy the succulent goodness of food; for loving hearts and skilled hands that prepare and display food in pleasing array, creating meals that satisfy the soul as well as the stomach. May we remember the Christ who blessed the wedding feast at Cana whenever we eat and drink with family and friends. May our bread recall for us his body given for us on a cross so that we might be reconciled with the universe. And at the end of our meals, may we be reminded of the coming of his kingdom, when everyone will be full from a festive banquet that never ends. But in the meantime, may we never forget those who do not enjoy our bounty, that we might always be willing to share with the "least" of your children. In the name of the One who is the Bread of Life we pray. Amen.

30. When Grace Is Rejected
Romero

The spirit of the Lord GOD is upon me,
　　because the LORD has anointed me;
he has sent me to bring good news to the
　　oppressed,
　　to bind up the brokenhearted,
to proclaim liberty to the captives,
　　and release to the prisoners;
to proclaim the year of the LORD's favor.

Isaiah 61:1–2a

As many of you as were baptized into Christ have clothed yourselves with Christ. There is no longer Jew or Greek, there is no longer slave or free, there is no longer male and female; for all of you are one in Christ Jesus. And if you belong to Christ, then you are Abraham's offspring, heirs according to the promise.

Galatians 3:27–29

Introduction

Oscar Romero's spiritual journey from reclusive conservative priest to liberal champion of the poor is movingly portrayed by Raul Julia in *Romero*. Because of Romero's conservatism, the rich land owners of El Salvador had breathed a sigh of relief when he was appointed Archbishop, whereas priests working with the poor were dismayed. Only an old friend, Father Grande, held out any hope for the ministry of the new Archbishop; he had faith in the capacity of his friend to grow. And grow the new Archbishop does, as one by one Romero witnesses the disappearance of his activist priests and parishioners. Some of the other bishops might salve their consciences by believing that the activists were all Communists, but he knows better. He begins to speak out against the death squads and the government's complicity in the escalating violence. This becomes costly, earning the prelate bitter criticism from the bishops of his own cabinet as well as from government and army officials. He is the target of death threats, and, in the case of the following scene, old friendships are jeopardized. The Archbishop had been close to Arista, a beautiful young mother and her aristocratic family, often dining in her family's mansion. But this was a friendship that could not transcend their growing religious and political differences.

The Scene

Arista comes to Oscar Romero to request that he baptize her baby. He is delighted. He tells her to check with his secretary for including the child in the next group of babies to be baptized. She pointedly says no to this, that she wants a private baptism for her child. Romero replies that with his frantic schedule this is no longer possible. All baptisms are public ones now. She scornfully replies that *her* child will not be baptized along with *Indians*. He says that is the way it is now. Embittered, she refuses to accept this, declaring that he has turned against his own kind.

Reflection on the Scene

The ancient prophet's vision of the poor receiving good news and the captives release from their bondage informed all of Oscar Romero's thought and action during the last years of his life. He had dwelt in blissful ignorance among the well-to-do of his society until his elevation to the archbishopric. This brought him away from his beloved books and into the dusty roads and blood-soaked fields of the common people. He saw firsthand what the terrible imbalance of wealth (a few hundred families owning 90 percent of the wealth of El Salvador) had done to his country. The apostle Paul's great vision of a classless people of God was not embodied in the present church, for it was as sharply divided as Salvadoran society. The church, instead of leading toward the prophet's and Paul's vision of a just and loving fellowship free from all differences of race, sex, or class, had become merely a reflection of fallen society, still replete with all its terrible injustices.

Arista, captive to the prejudice against and scorn for peasants and Indians held by members of her aristocratic class, refused to help or even mingle with them long enough for a baptismal service. She believed the sacrament to be a means of grace, but only for those who deserved it, members of her class. She could not accept it in the form offered by her friend because it threatened her value system, which was based on wealth, rank, and privilege, not love and justice. In rejecting the Archbishop's offer, she rejected the grace of God, the one thing that could free her from her prejudice and bigotry—indeed, the one thing that could free her whole country of its fratricidal hatred and killing.

For Further Reflection

1. Are there still traces of long-held prejudices in your heart that affect the way you value some people more than others?

2. What is the church in which you were baptized like? Is it a fellowship of mixed races and people from different cultural backgrounds, or is it "homogenized"? What has made most U.S. (and Canadian) churches attract only "their own kind"? If you belong to or know of a multiracial church, how does it work to maintain such a state?

3. When grace is spurned, what does God do? One answer is that God becomes angry and vents his wrath upon the person or group. What is the truth in the concept of "the wrath of God"? How is it often distorted by media preachers? What seems to be Christ's response to those who reject him, and thus grace? See Luke 23:34 for perhaps the ultimate answer to such a question.

4. Read or sing John Newton's great hymn "Amazing Grace." When you read or hear the hymn, what images of God come to mind? A shepherd? A loving parent reaching out to us? What feelings arise toward God? Toward other people? Are any class or

racial distinctions made in the song? If I am the recipient of such abundant grace, how am I going to regard others, especially those who are different? What can I do to embrace and cooperate with the apostle Paul's vision of a grace-filled fellowship?

HYMN: "Turn Back, O Man, Forswear Thy Foolish Ways" or "Amazing Grace"

A Prayer

Dear God, we often address you as "gracious," and so you are. You are ever more willing to accept us than we are to accept ourselves. You ever reach out and give more than we are willing or able to receive. In and through Christ's great sacrifice on the cross you claim us, call us, redeem us. In our own baptism you have gifted us with your gracious Spirit and commissioned us to be channels of that same grace. Continue to mold us by your Spirit, that we might become more gracious each day. Open our eyes and sensitize us to the way people are treated in our church, office, place of work or study, and our neighborhood. Draw us a little nearer each day to the ancient vision of a church and society in which there is no rich or poor, no gay or straight, no male or female, no white majority or racial minority. This we ask in the name of the One in whose death all differences are swept away by your river of grace. Amen.

31. A Place for Everyone
Places in the Heart

How good and pleasant it is
    when kindred live together in unity!
It is like the precious oil on the head,
    running down upon the beard,
on the beard of Aaron,
    running down over the collar of his robes.
It is like the dew of Hermon,
    which falls on the mountains of Zion.
For there the LORD ordained his blessing,
    life forevermore.

Psalm 133

If I speak in the tongues of mortals and of angels, but do not have love, I am a noisy gong or a clanging cymbal. And if I have prophetic powers, and understand all mysteries and all knowledge, and if I have all faith, so as to remove mountains, but do not have love, I am nothing. If I give away all my possessions, and if I hand over my body so that I may boast, but do not have love, I gain nothing.

1 Corinthians 13:1–3

Therefore, since we are surrounded by so great a cloud of witnesses, let us also lay aside every weight and the sin that clings so closely, and let us run with perseverance the race that is set before us, looking to Jesus the pioneer and perfecter of our faith, who for the sake of the joy that was set before him endured the cross, disregarding its shame, and has taken his seat at the right hand of the throne of God.

Hebrews 12:1–2

I believe in . . . the holy catholic Church, the communion of saints, the forgiveness of sins."

> The Apostles' Creed

Introduction

In Robert Benton's *Places in the Heart*, we watch a disparate and desperate group of Texans slowly become a family as they struggle toward a goal during the hard days of the Depression. Edna is widowed suddenly when her sheriff husband is accidentally shot by a drunken black teenager. The boy is lynched by her neighbors, and she is left with nothing but their mortgaged farm to make a living for herself and her young son and daughter, Frank and Possum. She accepts the offer of help from a black handyman, Moze, and against the advice of the banker holding the mortgage, decides to raise a crop of cotton. The banker forces her to take in his blind, unwanted brother-in-law, Will, as a boarder. Hostile at first, Will slowly begins to fit into the family, especially after a destructive tornado blows through the farm. He realizes how precious the children, whom he had regarded as nuisances, really are. At the crucial harvesttime, he does what he can to help out, as does Edna's sister Margaret and her husband, Wayne. The latter are going through their own crisis, Margaret discovering that Wayne was having an affair with the wife of their best friend. She allows the repentant Wayne to stay with her but angrily tells him he is never to touch her again.

At harvesttime, Edna and all join together to become the first to finish gathering the crop and delivering it to the local cotton gin. As Moze had counseled Edna, there is a hefty bonus for being first; the cash prize is just enough for her to save the farm and have enough to start another round of planting. Through tremendous effort they succeed, and Moze even manages to guide her through the process of negotiating a favorable price with the unscrupulous owner of the cotton gin. But Moze pays a price, for the Klan beats him and runs him out of town. But he leaves with the blessing of Edna, who assures him that no one else could have taken such an unlikely piece of land and unskilled workers and completed the harvest on time.

The Scene

The last scene in the film takes place in the little clapboard church of the village. The choir finishes a song, and the pastor reads from First Corinthians, chapter 13, "Though I speak in the tongues of men and of angels . . ." We see the estranged Wayne and Margaret sitting together, and yet not really together, until the truth of the apostle Paul's words apparently affects her. The camera shows us a close-up of her hand reaching over and clasping his. A smile of relief appears on Wayne's face. Caught up in Paul's beautiful words, Margaret allows the miracle of forgiveness to melt the cold, hostile wall she had erected between them.

Then we hear the strains of the hymn "In the Garden." The choir sings the words, which form the background to the pastor's voice. He is repeating again the familiar Words of Institution, also from Paul, that begin the sacrament of the Lord's Supper. The trays of bread and wine are then brought to the congregation, and each person takes them and passes the elements to a neighbor. Everyone is there, including the cruel town banker and the mill owner. Then we are brought up short—Moze is present! But he has left town, and even if he hadn't, he wouldn't dare come to a white church in 1930s Texas! The elements continue their passage around the congregation. The children receive them. Then Edna—she passes it to her husband! But he is dead! He passes it to the black teenager, also dead! The scene fades to black, with the hymn coming to its conclusion.

What is happening? We "see" in this scene that closes the film an even greater miracle than Margaret's forgiving Wayne—a miracle of faith.

Reflection on the Scene

Christians should be able to understand the marvelous, surrealistic Communion scene, because every time they join in declaring the Apostles' Creed or hear the Great Prayer during the Communion service, the belief in the communion of saints is affirmed. This belief that "a great cloud of witnesses" surround the Christian, especially during the celebration of the sacrament, is a basic one. All who have believed, who now believe, and who will believe, are gathered in faith to the Christ of the Holy Eucharist. The Christian is thus never alone. This is a belief that can bring us comfort, assurance, and challenge. In the simple service, Edna and her children are joined by all who are joined with them in Christ—her dead husband and Moze, even the boy killer, and the banker and the mill owner who claim belief but do not practice it. All are bound together in grace. It should be comforting for us to realize that our faith pilgrimage is never entered into alone, but that we have companions, visible and invisible, who walk with us. It is good to remember that the word *companion* derives from the French phrase meaning "one with whom one shares bread."

For Further Reflection

1. What is your own experience with the Lord's Supper? Do you feel at times a kinship with those who have gone before? How is the Supper more than just a memorial for a dead prophet? What has been your most memorable experience of the Eucharist?

2. How is harboring resentment of past wrongs injurious to one's well-being? What has happened to Margaret as a result of her attitude toward Wayne? What in the Scripture passage do you think spoke to her? How has the Scripture become a means of grace for her and Wayne? Have you had the experience of listening to a passage, perhaps a familiar one, and then feeling that the Holy Spirit was speaking through it directly to you and your situation?

3. How have you reacted toward others who have hurt or betrayed you? Are you able to forgive them? Does the liturgy of the Communion service aid in this process?

4. Sometimes young people are very resentful that director Benton included the banker and the mill owner in the Communion service. "They don't deserve to be there!" the young people exclaim in righteous indignation. What would you reply? Do any of us "deserve" to receive the sacrament? On what basis are we included? How is the sacrament "a means of grace"?

5. If you have seen the whole film, you might notice that it begins and ends with eating: the ending, of course, the Lord's Supper; and at the beginning a series of shots of people around the village eating their meals. What is the author saying about eating and the sacra-

ment? Is Christ present in the family meals also? How are tables in the home connected with the Lord's Table? Some liturgies include part of Luke's text of the Emmaus walk and meal as part of the Words of Institution. How does this add meaning to our everyday eating?

HYMN: "Blest Be the Tie that Binds" or "I Come with Joy"

A Prayer

Gracious God, giver of bread and wine, and indeed, of all our daily food, we give you thanks for the insights that can be gained from such a film as this one. We are grateful that you accept us as we are and change us through Christ and the Holy Spirit as we seek to live out our faith. Make us aware of your presence whenever we share bread with others, and keep us in a right relationship with our neighbors, even with those who have hurt or betrayed us. As Christ forgave, so enable us also to forgive. Make us open to the possibility of change for the better, within ourselves and within those in whom we least expect it. We pray this in the name of the transforming Christ. Amen.

Appendix

List of Films and Videocassette Companies

All of the following films should be available at most video stores or a public library.

American History X. New Line Home Video. Rated R. Tony Kaye, director. 1998. 117 minutes.

Babe: Pig in the City. MCA Universal Home Video. Rated G. George Miller, director. 1998. 97 minutes.

Babette's Feast. Orion Home Video (available in dubbed version). Rated G. Gabriel Axel, director. 1987. 102 minutes.

Beautiful Dreamers. Hemdale Home Video. Rated PG-13. John Kent Harrison, director. 1990. 105 minutes.

Charly. CBS Fox Video. Rated PG. Ralph Nelson, director. 1968. 103 minutes.

The Color Purple. Warner Home Video. Rated R. Steven Spielberg, director. 1985. 152 minutes.

Dead Man Walking. PolyGram Video. Rated R. Tim Robbins, director. 1995. 122 minutes.

The Deer Hunter. MCA Home Video. Rated R. Michael Cimino, director. 1978. 183 minutes.

Empire of the Sun. Warner Home Video. Rated PG. Steven Spielberg, director. 1987. 154 minutes.

Entertaining Angels: The Dorothy Day Story. Warner Home Video. Rated PG. Michael Ray Rhodes, director. 1996. 110 minutes.

Field of Dreams. MCA Home Video. Rated PG. Phil Alden Robinson, director. 1989. 107 minutes.

Grand Canyon. Fox Video. Rated R. Lawrence Kasden, director. 1991. 134 minutes.

The Great Santini. Warner Home Video. Rated PG. Lewis John
  Carlino, director. 1979. 115 minutes.
Les Miserables. Columbia TriStar Home Video. Rated PG-13.
  Richard Boleslawski, director. 1935. 108 minutes.
Marvin's Room. Miramax Video. Rated PG-13. Jerry Zaks, director.
  1996. 98 minutes.
The Mission. Warner Home Video. Rated PG. Roland Joffe, direc-
  tor. 1986. 126 minutes.
Out of Africa. MCA Home Video. Rated PG. Sydney Pollack,
  director. 1985. 150 minutes.
Places in the Heart. CBS Fox Video. Rated PG. Robert Benson,
  director. 1984. 112 minutes.
Pulp Fiction. Miramax Home Entertainment. Rated R. Quentin
  Tarantino, director. 1994. 154 minutes.
The River. MCA Home Video. Rated PG-13. Mark Rydell, direc-
  tor. 1984. 122 minutes.
Romero. Vidmark Entertainment. Rated PG-13. John Duigan,
  director. 1989. 102 minutes.
Saturday Night Fever. Paramount Home Video. Rated R. John
  Badham, director. 1977. 118 minutes.
Schindler's List. MCA Universal Home Video. Rated R. Steven
  Spielberg, director. 1993. 197 minutes.
The Shawshank Redemption. Warner Home Video. Rated R. Frank
  Darabont, director. 1994. 142 minutes.
Smoke. Miramax Home Entertainment. Rated R. Wayne Wang,
  director. 1995. 112 minutes.
The Spitfire Grill. Columbia TriStar Home Video. Rated PG-13.
  Lee David Zlotoff, director. 1996. 117 minutes.
Star Wars. CBS Fox Video. Rated PG. George Lucas, director.
  1977. 121 minutes.
Tender Mercies. HBO Video. Rated PG. Bruce Beresford, director.
  1983. 92 minutes.
To Kill a Mockingbird. MCA Home Video. Not Rated. Robert
  Mulligan, director. 1962. 129 minutes.
The War. MCA Home Video. Rated PG-13. John Avnet, dir. 1994.
  127 minutes.

A Note About:
Reel to Real

All those working with youth will want to obtain this beautifully produced quarterly magazine that explores through film and the Scriptures issues of great interest to youth. Wrapped in a four-color heavy-stock cover, each issue includes designs for a retreat, youth meetings of one to five or more sessions, and a devotional. For further information write: *Reel to Real*, United Methodist Board of Publications, P.O. Box 801, Nashville, TN 37202-0801. You can also check at your local Cokesbury Bookstore.

Visual Parables

Those who want to keep up with current films and find the precious off-beat gems that receive little publicity will want to consider subscribing to *Visual Parables*. The author reviews films and videos from a theological perspective each month. Each issue of thirty pages or more also contains reviews of film books, a film discussion/reflection guide, film articles, a lectionary-related column of film illustrations, and, of course, the feature "Praying the Movies." For a free sample copy, call Robin Kash at 800-528-6522. The author may be reached by E-mail for questions about films or his film seminars at mcnulty@catskill.net.

Peacemaking Materials

Many of the meditations in this book are concerned with peacemaking issues. Lack of space prevents us from dealing with these issues in more detail. Those who want to delve deeper would do well to get in touch with the Presbyterian Peacemaking Program, which publishes a shelf-full of excellent peacemaking Bible studies and curriculum materials for children, youth, and adults. They also hold a national Peacemaking Conference each year. Write: Presbyterian Peacemaking Office, 100 Witherspoon Street, Louisville, KY 40202-1396.

Building a Video Library

The films in this book would make a fine core collection of films for a church library. The church would make them more accessible to members and to its classes and groups. A church in Connecticut copies the reviews of and guides for the film from Visual Parables and indicates this on the library card for the film. Thus the borrowers have some information setting forth the theological content of the film.